LANGUAGE
OF THE
HEART

Carolyn Pogue

LANGUAGE
OF THE
HEART

RITUALS
STORIES AND
INFORMATION
ABOUT
DEATH

Northstone

Editors: Michael Schwartzentruber, Dianne Greenslade
Cover design: Margaret Kyle
Interior design: Julie Bachewich
Consulting art director: Robert MacDonald
Cover artwork: public domain, colored by Margaret Kyle

Permissions:
Quotation from *Services for Death and Burial: for Optional Use in the
United Church of Canada,* published by the Division of Mission in Canada,
The United Church of Canada, copyright 1987, used by permission.
"Prayer at Death," excerpted from *Canadian Church Diary 1997,*
copyright 1997, used by permission.

Northstone Publishing Inc. is an employee-owned company, committed to caring for the
environment and all creation. Northstone recycles, reuses and composts, and encourages
readers to do the same. Resources are printed on recycled paper and more environmentally
friendly groundwod papers (newsprint), whenever possible. The trees used are replaced
through donations to the Scoutrees for Canada Program.
Ten percent of all profit is donated to charitable organizations.

Canadian Cataloguing in Publication Data
Pogue, Carolym, 1948
Language of the heart
Includes bibliographical references and index.
ISBN 1-896836-17-8
1. Funeral rites and ceremonies. I. Title.
GT3213.A2P66 1998   393.9   C97-911086-6

Published by Northstone Publishing Inc.

Printing
9 8 7 6 5 4 3 2

Printed in Canada by Transcontinental Printing Inc.
Louiseville, Quebec

I have always known
That at last
I would take this road.
But yesterday,
I did not know
It would be today.

Ariwara Narihira
823-880

Contents

Acknowledgments 9

Introduction 11

ONE Where We Stand Today 15

TWO Practical Matters 33

THREE A Funeral Home – or Not 57

FOUR Planning a Ceremony 71

FIVE The Death of a Child 101

SIX Suicide 119

SEVEN Your Own Death 135

EIGHT Legal and Financial Matters 149

NINE Transplants and Organ Donation 159

Afterword 169

Appendix A: Resources 171

Appendix B: Suggested Scripture Readings 185

Index 191

Acknowledgments

One day, when I was minding my own business, Michael Schwartzentruber at Northstone Publishing telephoned and asked me to write this book. It took several days to come to the decision to go ahead. Seven months later, I am grateful.

It's been a wild ride. Walking into funeral parlors "stone cold sober" has been interesting. Reading about mourning, death, and funeral practices has been eye-popping, and affirming. But when I listened to people's stories about their experiences with death, I knew I was standing on holy ground.

During these months, family, friends and strangers asked me what I was doing. "Writing a book about funerals," I answered. The response was usually a moment of silence. I wondered if they were wishing I'd said something else, like I was writing a romantic novel or a poem or a book about ducks. Anything. But then often, these strangers, friends and family members told me a story about a very good funeral they'd attended or a very bad one.

The storytellers include Jan Bjorkman, Georgia Black, Michele Bland, Sophie Borcoman, John Branton, Marty Brown, Doug Cowan, Debbie Culbertson, Anne Davies, Francie Hagedorn, Lois Harding, Marian Hood, Alyson Huntly, Lindy Jones, Audrey Kaldestad, Anne Klaiber, Ursula Lewis, Chris Levan, Leah-Ann Lymer, Barb McConnell, Catherine MacLean, Claire McMordie, Clint Mooney, Debbie Morrison, Ruth Newell, Marilyn Perkins, Cheryl Perry, Clayton Pogue, Betty Norris Rykes, Marie Saretsky, James Taylor, Erica Tesar, Bert White, Tony Wright, Val Wright, Lora Wyman, and people on buses, planes and at the hairdresser's. Thank you for your trust.

I am grateful to Brent Forrester, Ernie Hagel, Margaret Hall, Marion McGuigan, Susan Murphy, Bill Phipps, Carolyn Ryder, Anne Sanders, and David Sellick for answering specific questions.

I am indebted to Jean Blacklock, Bill Hodgins, Laurie Mader, Sheena Meurin, Kim Roach, and The Pleasant Heights Discussion Group for reading portions of the manuscript.

For reading the entire manuscript, loving thanks to Bill Phipps, Ruth Pogue, Clayton Pogue and Kathy Bach Paterson.

Introduction

When I was in my early 20s, I moved next door to Mary, a woman recently widowed. Many afternoons or evenings we'd sit on her deck overlooking Great Slave Lake and she would talk about what had happened. She told me stories about her husband's heart attack, his stay in hospital, how he'd died and been resuscitated, what he saw when he was dead. She talked about the gift of his final year after that attack and how their discussions deepened their love and prepared her for his final departure.

Several times during the telling of those stories she remarked, "You're so young to be hearing all this. I shouldn't be telling you." And then she'd recall another story and keep talking. I knew, even then, that I was hearing sacred stories.

Over the years I've thought of her and silently thanked her. The toddler who sometimes played or slept nearby when she was talking – my son Michael – died less than 20 years later.

I remembered Mary while I sat in Michael's hospital room that day in December 1991. I believe that her telling somehow prepared me.

Michael was dying, the doctor told me. There was no use thinking otherwise. My purpose for being in his room was not to beg him to live, but to be with him when he left this world. My husband Bill and our friend Betty were with me.

When we entered the room, Betty laid her hand on his head and blessed him using the ancient Hebrew text, "May the Lord bless you and keep you; May the Lord be kind and gracious to you; May the Lord look on you with favor and give you peace" (Numbers 6:24–26).

In the hours that followed, she also sang in Cree, her first language.

She said that she was "singing him to the other side." Michael's heritage was Slavey. Betty, a Métis, was like a bridge for us in many ways.

I've been told we were there about five hours. But time, for me, was meaningless, suspended by the force of shock and love. I floated inside the eye of a hurricane. The room was an island apart from the rest of the world.

I remember stroking his arm and chest, holding his hand, touching his face. I remember loving him and telling him that – over and over and over. Bill and I named the other members of our family who loved him and were with him. In truth, I don't know how much I said out loud, and how much was in my mind. I only know that I was as present to him then as ever I've been. I remember Betty telling me to let him go. "Say it!" she said. "He's trying to hang on for you." When he stopped breathing, I didn't notice at first. Betty had to tell me.

We all left the room and the attendant who had been, I think, unobtrusively present throughout, closed the curtains around his bed. I walked into the hall, and then needed to go back. The attendant looked guilty when I returned. "I was just lowering the bed," he said. I didn't care. I just had to touch my son one more time. I had to be sure, I guess.

This is a book about one aspect of life about which many of us feel shy and awkward. Reverend Audrey Kaldestad of Westlock, Alberta says that when she was a child she was taught it was impolite to discuss religion, politics or sex because these were topics likely to cause upset. "Nowadays the only tabu subject is death. One would think most of us were not eventually going to die."

This is a book of courage. The stories in this book are told by people who have looked death in the face. Some of the stories include the particular rituals they used to help them. Some of the stories tell how people midwife the bereaved to life on the other side of that river of sadness that seems so wide.

This is a book that will encourage you to do whatever you need to do, rather than what you think is expected of you. Too many of us endure meaningless ceremonies that add to our grief, rather than help us make a healthy transition.

It contains sample rituals and ceremonies that you might adapt for your own use in planning your own funeral ceremony, or in planning a memorial or healing ritual for a death that is long past.

There is practical advice from people who have "been there, done that." There are stories of women, children and men who have lost a loved one, or not so loved one, through death. A whole chapter of answers to questions about *what happens, really*, will prepare you for the inevitable day you will make decisions for yourself or for another. Other sections offer advice on legal and financial matters, stories about organ donations, about death by suicide, the death of children (adult, young or unborn). One chapter "walks" you through a funeral home, then includes stories about how some people arrange funerals without one.

I hope that this book will present new possibilities and open imaginations to how things could be. Many of us have the idea that at funerals or memorials or celebrations of life there must be clergy, there must be organ music and so on. But other possiblities exist if we use our imaginations.

One of the more interesting memorial services I learned about took place one evening in Field, British Columbia. Children and adults sat on logs and stumps outside within the bosom of the Rocky Mountains. Sophie Borcoman and friends conducted the service and included a reading from an Environment Canada manual, a eulogy, a poem, some silence, and some discussion. It was for two grizzly bears.

In a wonderful book called *Bears* by Kevin Van Tighem (Canmore: Altitude Publishing, 1997). I had read the story of how the town residents became acquainted with two grizzlies they named Field and Sissy. We visited Sophie in her home in Field last summer. She told us that it was not unusual to see the bears sitting on someone's lawn eating dandelions. People and bears kept their distance.

In the end, though, Sissy was killed on the highway by a tour bus. Field discovered garbage and eventually had to be destroyed. The ceremony, Sophie told me, gave people an opportunity to voice their sorrow and anger about the loss of their wild friends and to raise awareness of the fact that grizzlies are in trouble. Today, in the Rockies, only half the land mass necessary for their habitat remains.

I hope that this book, like Sophie's straightforward compassionate act, offers an opportunity to examine some of our assumptions about life and death. Although many of our traditions, rituals and ceremonies have been given away or buried under denial and superficiality and stiff upper lips, I think we can reclaim them and make them our own again.

Calgary, Canada

ONE

WHERE WE STAND TODAY

The most important thing about life is that it is limited.
People who face this do better
psychologically and spiritually
than those who ignore or deny it.
Author Scott Peck,
on CBC Radio January, 1997

This century has changed how and where people live. A few generations ago, most of us lived in the country. Now most of us live in cities and towns. I am typical of my generation – raised on a small mixed farm, living now in a large city. When I compare myself at ten years of age with a child in my current neighborhood, I see that our realities are different. She knows how to surf the Internet, but has never seen a cow slaughtered, a kitten born, a piglet suckled. She can program a VCR, but has never conducted a funeral for a hankie-wrapped frog or her faithful old collie.

This century has changed how and where people die, too. Because people live longer, many of us reach middle age without having arranged, or even attended, a funeral. Once, most of us died at home; we knew about death because we saw it up close. Today, 80 percent of us die in an institution. Most of us view death through the wrong end of binoculars – at a distance.

Even when the very old or very ill are facing death and want to discuss it, we get nervous and change the subject, depriving them and ourselves of exploration, education and intimacy. Death is often viewed as an aberration – we have failed at keeping it away.

Once I was in the company of a woman whose grandmother had died. A friend joined us and said, "I'm so sorry to hear about your grandmother." The woman thanked him for his concern. He then asked the grandmother's age. "Ninety-six," came the answer. "What did she die of?" he asked. I've been laughing at the answer for years. "Of being 96!" replied the woman.

When the phone call comes, we are seldom prepared. When the

doctor says, "There is nothing more we can do," most of us ritually shake our heads and utter, "No," feeling more lonely and vulnerable than we ever imagined.

Our society works hard at denying death. When it comes, we are in a crisis and bewilderment – even when the deceased is of a great age. Many of us panic. And it is in this state that we make decisions that will affect us the rest of our lives – perhaps financially, certainly emotionally.

Not only do we try to deny death, but our society works hard at controlling life. We invent machinery to prolong it, to rescue fetuses and to try to work miracles to "bring people back." We fear losing control.

Denial and control are important cultural values, it seems. Face-lifts and creams, flattering clothes and hair dye, cosmetics and hair-grow tonics promise to "fight" the aging process.

Our denial extends, of course, to Earth. We don't even believe that the Earth can die. That is why strip mining, clear-cutting, mega-farming and drag-netting still go on. As a society, we don't actually want to believe in death. We don't want to believe it can happen to us.

Maybe death frightens us to the point of denial because we know that we will die in our own company, and perhaps we don't know who "me" is. We live alienated from ourselves, aided and abetted by too much television, too much noise, too much busy-ness. But no matter how rich or young or creative or clever we are, we will die. Death isn't an option!

When my friend was learning to live with cancer she said, "I learned to appreciate the smallest, simplest pleasures – a child's laughter, a sunset, a cup of tea. Yes, it was terrible and a shock and painful. But it [cancer] gave me gifts, too. I take nothing for granted now. I learned to *live*!" My friend had ended her alienation from herself and discovered simple living.

Simplicity

Today, some people are rethinking their lives, making decisions to simplify them and to live out their true values. Some head for the hills to raise goats because the rat race is too soul-destroying. Some strip down celebrations such as Christmas in order to opt out of the consumer-oriented noise that replaces peace and renewal. "Voluntary simplicity," is a term applied to the movement away from materialistic values to an inwardly more rich lifestyle.

Voluntary simplicity reaches into all aspects of living. It can also help us with the business of dying, and with the ceremonies and rituals we use to help us. "Simplicity in [funeral] arrangements can effect great economy, but even more importantly it can help center attention on spiritual values and the life of the person who has died, rather than on material things," writes Ernest Morgan in *Dealing Creatively with Death*.

Perhaps we can learn (or relearn) to see life in a different light. Perhaps we can willingly see it as a full circle, of which death is a part. But intellectual knowledge differs from emotional acceptance. We need tools to help us understand change. Rituals and ceremonies are tools for change.

Rituals and Ceremonies

Ever since the Industrial Revolution, much of our secular society has shunned rituals as magic or superstitious nonsense that we could do very well without if we used logic, science and common sense. But throwing away so many of our rituals can leave us naked. Although some of life is logical, much of it is not. Even the young understand that life is full of mystery. Without rituals and ceremonies within our communities and families, we feel adrift and cannot understand why.

The funerals of Mother Teresa in Calcutta and Princess Diana in

London in September 1997 perhaps reminded us of the importance of ritual. Their funerals, watched by millions of people throughout the world, became an opportunity to participate in rituals, remembrance and public mourning on a global scale. In our society, crying and wailing are often considered bad taste. But during those funerals and the week leading up to them, millions expressed their grief openly. We have been helped, I hope, to move away from feeling that it's "bad manners" to show grief in public.

When our meaningful rituals and ceremonies are given away to hospitals and funeral homes, we can find ourselves unable to adjust, or bewildered by our feelings.

More people today seem interested in paying attention to personal and community rituals and ceremonies. Further, they are exploring their meanings.

Marie Saretsky, a Saskatchewan artist, creates paper products and dried flower arrangements. The mountains of flowers offered not only in London and Calcutta, but in countries from Indonesia to Australia to Canada did not surprise her. She says that the ritual of using flowers at times of death is nothing new. Thousands of years ago, people placed handfuls of flowers on graves in Asia. Flower wreaths (circles being the symbol for eternity and wholeness) were used in funerals in Egypt 4,500 years ago. Some of our rituals are so old they seem bred in our very bones.

When we use rituals, we use the language of the heart. When couples exchange rings they are symbolizing unending love and loyalty – and more than words can express. When Christians eat bread and drink wine, they nourish not their bodies, but their souls. When the Sister of Charity carried a pencil past Mother Teresa's open coffin, it symbolized Mother Teresa's philosophy: "I am a pencil in the hand of God." When bells toll slowly, they sing a lament.

According to Kathleen Wall and Gary Ferguson, authors of *Lights of Passage*, "Rituals carry us into the belly of the change process, encouraging us to embrace [the change] rather than become distracted or run away." They say that ritual works in three basic ways: "It empowers us through action, it clarifies problems and new directions, and it helps new perspectives and behaviors take root in our daily lives."

In North America, religious institutions and Elders have been and still are, the "keepers of the rituals." In rethinking our values, and stripping down to what is essential for spiritual development, more of us want to participate in rituals and ceremonies that mean something to us. Death ceremonies are changing.

Funerals in North America

Early settlers on the continent reenacted what they knew from their country of origin: the community gathered, the men built a casket or hired a carpenter for the job, and dug the grave. It was the responsibility of the women to prepare the body for burial and to line the casket. The body remained at home until the funeral, and people took turns sitting with it around the clock. The casket was transported by wagon to the church, and buried in the church yard.

Even 40 years ago, funerals in smalltown Ontario were different from today. John Branton recalls that when his mother died, she was brought home from the hospital and her coffin remained in the living room, with someone always in attendance, for the three days before the funeral. He recalls the symbols present – the wreath on the door announcing that his family was in mourning, the candles burning in the living room. He remembers the house filling with neighbors and relatives praying the rosary, some on their knees, some sitting, some standing. He recalls the food brought by the community. These symbols and rituals for the dead in his home had a profound effect on him. They made him feel personally embraced by the community with warmth and love.

Of course, not all ceremonies like this are a thing of the past. In

Hutterite communities, in some rural areas and in the North, for example, there is still a great deal of community participation. In Fort Smith, NWT, the body of the deceased may be transported in the back of a pickup truck, with family and friends riding along in the back. While the men of Rankin Inlet, NWT, build a casket as needed, the women take responsibility for the preparation of the body for burial. This preparation means washing, dressing and combing the hair of the deceased.

Funeral directors appeared on the scene in North America about 1900. Over the century, the casket in the front parlor of the home is being or has been gradually replaced with the casket on display in a funeral parlor. Funeral directors took over the job of preparing the body. Funeral homes began to provide transportation. As church cemeteries filled, the municipality took over as owner and keeper of vast tracts of land within cities. It became the job of cemetery workers to dig the grave and later to cover it. Embalming was introduced. Although no law in Canada or the United States requires embalming (except in certain cases), it has become a generally accepted procedure. Make-up artists were trained in the fine art of making a corpse look alive. Flowers grew into big business, caskets became more ornate and expensive, caterers appeared. In short, the bereaved, whether by design or by accident lost hands-on involvement in preparing for the burial – except to write the checks for flowers, the monument, the coffin, the obituary, the caterer and the burial plot. At worst, the community's involvement consists mainly of writing a sympathy card.

Brent Forrester of Thompson Funeral Home in Aurora, Ontario, says funerals have changed even in the past ten years. "There's no such thing anymore as a traditional funeral," he says. "There are fewer funerals [ceremonies with the body present] and more memorializations, fewer flowers and more gifts in memory of the deceased. Because people better understand the grief of children, they are more often included in the preparation and planning. I think [the ceremonies] are changing to make them more unique to the deceased and more meaningful for the family."

A brochure from The Memorial Society of Madison, Wisconsin, says that with the spread of the hospice movement, families are assuming more responsibility at the time of death, and home or church funerals are again returning.

A better understanding of cultures different from our own also means change. In her booklet, *Customs and Traditions in Times of Death and Bereavement*, Kathy Cloutier includes the rites of the Blackfoot, Buddhist, Chinese, Mormon, Eastern Orthodox, Hindu, Hutterite, Muslim, Jehovah Witness, Sikh and more. Learning about other customs can help us better understand our own and can teach us about commonalities that unite the human family. It opens us to the experience of others.

Our Feelings

Experience, literature, Hollywood films, and, since 1997, televised funeral services such as Mother Teresa's and Princess Diana's shape our opinions about funerals. What child can forget the cellar where poor, orphaned Oliver Twist was held captive among the caskets by a ghoulish undertaker? (The first time I went into a funeral home to choose a coffin, I fully expected to be led down some rickety steps into a cobwebby, dank cellar. I was shocked – and relieved – to enter a carpeted, brightly lit room on the main floor!) Who will forget whispering the Lord's Prayer at 4:00 a.m. in Canada, along with millions of people in England and throughout the world, as we witnessed Princess Diana's funeral?

Hollywood stereotypes "men of the cloth" (few women clergy have made it to the big screen so far) into caricatures who *intone* rather than speak, and who parrot lines that make them either super- or sub-humans who do not feel or think at all like the rest of us, and who are caught up in some 1950s twilight zone of unreality. Whether they are marrying or burying, Hollywood "clergy" are seldom portrayed as people who are compassionate, creative, humorous or feminist. Obviously, the weddings and funerals performed by these cartoons are cartoons in themselves, but they may be all we know until someone close to us dies.

National Geographic-type magazines and some television documentaries offer us the unusual or the exotic. Last year, I watched a documentary on an educational network. A villager in Africa makes caskets to fulfill the dreams of the deceased. I watched in wonder and amazement as an American journalist interviewed him standing in front of a partially finished casket which was in the shape of a Cadillac, complete with chrome and headlights. "It's what he always wanted," explained the translator.

Our personal experience may have included attending a funeral when we were very young with an adult who didn't take the time to help us understand what was going on. I attended the funeral of a distant relative when I was five, accompanied by my uncle. (The one who used to push out his false teeth and make them snap in the air.) I was flabbergasted at seeing the old lady lying in state with all the people in black tiptoeing around the *millions* of flowers. I was curious to see her – a stranger to me – and I was amazed, even then, at my uncle's irreverence. He cracked jokes!

If the first funeral you attend is for someone very close, the experience can be horrendous. Brent Forrester comments that attending a funeral for someone a little more distanced – a colleague at work, for example – can help you. "This pays off," he says, "because when people have been to a funeral they gain life experience. People seem more able to deal with arranging one for someone close if they at least know what to expect."

When Cheryl Perry was a youth group leader in Victoria, British Columbia, she took this idea a step further. "I phoned a funeral home and asked if I could bring my group for a tour. I interviewed the funeral director first so I'd know what to expect. She was terrific. We told the kids that they could ask anything they wanted, even if they thought it was a dumb question. It's one of the best things I've done with them. We got into all kinds of discussion." I have no doubt those teenagers are now better prepared than many adults and have a better idea of the kind of input they can have into arranging a death ceremony.

Attending a funeral conducted by someone who did not know the deceased can be disconcerting, and one can leave the ceremony feeling angry and bewildered. Attending a funeral that seems ostentatious or glitzy can also be upsetting.

If the deceased was an atheist or agnostic, an overtly religious ceremony can be a frustrating, hypocritical and sorrowful affair. Mourners' minds and hearts are appalled that the death they have come to mourn, or the life they have come to celebrate, is thwarted by an evangelist hell-bent on conversion.

Although most people still call in clergy (or ask the funeral director to call one), once in a while someone else conducts the funeral. According to Brent, this person acts rather like a facilitator, moderator, or master of ceremonies. It is someone who opens and closes the service, introduces someone to deliver an eulogy, and perhaps reads some poetry or prayers.

"I know that occasionally people complain that the minister didn't conduct a funeral well, but I see the other side. If the family had no church connection, why would they expect a clergy person to come in and conduct a nonreligious ceremony? The ceremony should be true to the deceased, but if you're asking someone who is obviously religious, you have to expect some sort of religious rite."

A strong ceremony that reflects the person is compassionate to those who loved that person. We can be uplifted and comforted by a ceremony where we can cry in the presence of people who care, where there is an opportunity for spiritual comfort and some good old-fashioned storytelling.

What Are Funerals For, Anyway?

There is more to a funeral or memorial than disposal of the body. No matter how "unreligious" we think we are, we are more than flesh and bone.

Current literature on grief tells us that grief cannot be avoided altogether. It may be postponed, it may even be softened, but in the end, it cannot be dismissed or avoided. For survivors, the ceremony at death is the beginning of a different life.

Just as one may pass through certain stages upon learning of impending death, there are stages through which people may pass in coming to terms with loss. Briefly, these are denial, anger, shock, bargaining, depression and acceptance. These feelings do not necessarily flow in a nice, neat order, but we shouldn't be surprised when or if they appear.

Funeral or memorial ceremonies can serve specific purposes. Above all, they provide a publicly-sanctioned opportunity for expressing mourning.

They can assist us in acknowledging the death. When we are not in the midst of bereavement shock, it may seem simple to acknowledge that someone has died. But in the throes of it, it is a different matter. While we may acknowledge the death with our minds, we need a way to acknowledge it at the deeper level – that of the heart. Author Dr. Elisabeth Kübler-Ross says in her book, *Questions and Answers on Death and Dying*, that a simple ritual is necessary to publicly and openly face the reality of death.

Ceremonies can help people express pain. There are few times and places in our society where this is acceptable. Accepting the loss and facing the reality of death is a process. A funeral or memorial service can help us begin that process in a healthy way, supported by people who love us.

Ceremonies can help us remember. The ritual helps us make the shift from living with the person to living with memories of the person. This is why storytelling during and after the ceremony can help us. In addition to the stories, pictures and mementos can help us. I attended the funeral of a geologist whose long life had included time in the Northwest Territories and worldwide travel. After the funeral, the assembly met his family for the traditional coffee and tea. Over two or three tables they had lovingly displayed photographs of his life and work, rock samples of which he was particularly proud and other mementos of his love, his family, and his work as a geologist. It felt good looking at all those pieces of his life.

Ceremonies help each of us reconsider our own values and the way we live. Every one of us will lose someone we love sometime. And every one of us will die. Rituals around death can help us affirm life, and pledge to live more fully this day and the next. Death is important to us because life is important to us.

Ceremonies can help us connect with our community. We need our community to help hold us up, and to help us re-create ourselves after loss. How many people say, "I don't know what to do or say in the face of this?" Attending the funeral can be a good place to begin. By your presence, you say, "You are not alone."

Ceremonies can also help us remember that we are a human family. Writing of the death of a friend, Father Bert White of Kent, England, recalls:

"One by one, they came to the front – Muslim, Jew, Hindu, Sikh and Christian. One by one they read their prayers and sacred stories with a somberness and sadness befitting the occasion. Yet, this sorrow was not one which sensed defeat or being overwhelmed. It was a sweet sorrow which celebrated life in death, light in darkness and which said, somehow, that all is well."

This was the funeral of Margot Kane, self-confessed atheist and former Catholic, who had devoted her life to justice and liberation for all. She worked with asylum-seekers to Britain.

"It would not be an exaggeration to say that most were awestruck by the experience of that unique gathering," says Bert. "Margot had achieved what bishops and popes had been unable to do. Within our own tradition, we've tried for years to coax and cajole Christians to get together in dialogue and to worship with people of other faiths, giving all the 'right' reasons for doing so. But it took the life story of an atheist to bring us together in a shared service. At her death, this was Margot's last great gift – to gather and unite these faith traditions of the world. It was a rare gift from a rare woman."

Ceremonies can help communities heal, too. Few Canadians are unaware of the 1992 mine disaster in Yellowknife, NWT, where nine men died in an underground bomb blast. Although most of the men were from "outside" – that is, from southern Canada, and so were returned to the province of origin for burial or cremation – the community, rocked to its foundations by this tragedy, needed to mourn before they could begin to heal.

Reverend Catherine MacLean of Yellowknife United Church was present when the disaster occurred, and was instrumental in helping to construct a memorial service.

"We had been doing some interfaith services of reconciliation throughout the strike, and we worked together to plan the memorial service at the time of the explosion and at the service we had a year later. We attempted to get people to recognize that we were still a community. Even if we didn't know personally the nine people who died, we were still part of the community, we all lived and breathed the same air."

In a city of 15,000, about 3,000 people attended the initial memorial service held in the community arena. Community participation and symbols were important. A miner's hat rested on a rock cairn at the front. A youth choir and local folk group provided music. Mel Brown, retired mine safety inspector, read *Heart o' the North,* by Robert W. Service. Yellowknife artist Janice Brown Daly created the art for the service folder. Nine roses, representing the nine men, and a tenth rose, placed by guests from Westray Mine in Nova Scotia (where a mine disaster had also occurred), were in view.

"Before the benediction," Catherine recalls, "we turned on the light on the miner's helmet. The miners' names were read, and then prayers were offered for the bereaved families, for our community, for peace and healing. We ended with The Lord's Prayer."

A year later, when little apparent progress had been made in labor relations, and when feelings about the explosion and the strike had not abated, another service was held in the community. The deep feelings were recognized and the desire for real healing was articulated. Yellowknife United Church invited the community to a worship service of Hope and Healing. It happened to be during the Ten Days of Repentance, between Rosh Hashanah and Yom Kippur. Catherine recalls that "a gift the Jewish community made to the service was the message that repentance and forgiveness reestablish our oneness with God. They offered a responsive litany seeking atonement."

They lit a large candle at the end of the service, and carried it outside. It was October; the land was preparing for the dark subarctic winter. A relay team left town and carried that candle for four kilometers to Giant Mine, site of the disaster and ongoing strike. Ever so carefully, the two-meter high candle was placed on a rock cairn near the mine. A Plexiglas windshield protected its delicate flame. During the memorial service, Catherine had invited the community to help keep the flame lit. "I asked them to look for it every time they drove out the Ingraham Trail, and if it had gone out, to stop and relight it. You know, every time I went past, it was lit." People cared about that little light in the midst of a horrendous murder investigation, in the midst of grief, in the midst of shock, media attention, and the ongoing strike. It burned through the dark winter days and nights until the strike ended in April, 1994.

Public or private, single or multiple, large or small, rituals can help us bend, rather than break, when the winds of change assail us.

Simple Lessons

We do not need elaborate ceremonies or elaborate caskets, flower displays or monuments. We need not give in to our family's or society's pressure to spend extravagantly or to endure a meaningless ceremony. We need a ceremony that means something to us and that sets us on a healthy path for grieving the loss. By reexamining our values and doing what we need to do, rather than what we think is expected of us, perhaps we can better accept that death is part of the circle of life.

I learned lessons in simplicity from visiting two public memorials. One was the Vietnam War Memorial in Washington, D.C. The memorial bears the names of the missing and the dead. The monument is unadorned marble. People come by the thousands to walk, to think, to pray, to remember, and sometimes to leave a memento to the memory of a friend, family member or even a stranger. It is a memorial profound in its simplicity.

The other memorial is at *Yad Vashem*, the Holocaust Memorial in Jerusalem. One building is in memory of the one million children murdered during the Holocaust. I entered the building on a walkway which has a handrail. As I proceeded along the walk, the room became progressively darker. I could hear first a woman's voice, and then a man's, speaking the name of a murdered child, naming the child's home town and age at death. In the center of the room one single candle bravely defied the darkness. Its light was reflected by what seemed like hundreds of mirrors so that the overall effect was that the light went on forever. I felt like I was above Earth; I felt rooted at the same time. It was awesome.

Conclusion

As we turn the pages of our lives, we never really know what words will greet us. It could be birth – of a baby, an idea, a song. It could be death. We do know that we are constantly changed by the words and events that eventually become our book of life. There are two languages on every page: the language of the mind, and the language of the heart. In our complicated world, much of life is written in the language of the mind. The message of death, however, is spoken in the language of the heart.

Living simply, examining our values, understanding our rituals can all help us write richer, more satisfying stories of our lives than our culture currently models. We can live more fully today. When death becomes part of the story, we can meet it with integrity.

In preparation for that meeting, Chapter 2 provides practical answers to many questions that will arise.

TWO

PRACTICAL MATTERS

A funeral or memorial ceremony
gives us an opportunity to reflect on our own values.
What is important to us?
At times of death, we ask questions,
including where our lives fit into the overall picture.
Death strips us, at least for a while,
of all the extraneous in our lives.
Bill Phipps, minister

Death

What are the rituals when a person is in the process of dying?
In Appendix B, you will find suggested prayers from the Anglican and
United Church of Canada traditions. Reading these will give you an
idea of what professional clergy might do at that time.

I would say that if you have the opportunity, courage and compassion
to enter into the presence of a dying person, you will know what to do
by instinct. For example, you will likely want to hold the person you
love. You will likely want to say "I love you," and reassure the person
by your presence. You will likely want to hold the person's hand and
stroke it. Your deepest feelings, your deepest memories will surface.
You will likely cry. You will likely remember. You will likely feel that
this is a sacred, intimate moment in life – a moment out of time.

My husband, Bill, was with his mother when she died. His story of
this time is one of the reasons I fell in love with him, in fact. He says
that his mother was very small, and that he was able to hold her and
caress her. He held her close to him and spoke into her ear, giving her
a litany in effect, of all the people who loved her and were with her. He
said it was important not to feel rushed, but to take as much time
afterward as he wanted. After she died, he stayed and spent a long time
just being and thinking and remembering.

When my friend's mother died after a long hospitalization, she and
her family were with her. Shortly after death, the family called their
minister, who came immediately. With some of the long-term nurses

who had worked with and loved this woman, they prayed together. Their minister read a short passage that was relevant to the deceased, and talked a little about her life. It lasted less than ten minutes, but was a helpful interlude between death and the preparations for the formal memorial service.

The main advice from people who've been there is to take as much time as is necessary to do or say whatever you need. Do not stay away. Remember that it is believed that even unconscious people can hear.

When death occurs, what happens first?

This depends on where the death occurs. If the person died in an institution such as a hospital, a doctor will confirm the death and take care of the required paper work. The body will be taken to the hospital morgue until they are told by a funeral director or by you where you want the body taken.

If the person dies unexpectedly at home or anywhere a physician was not present, you need to phone emergency (911) so that a doctor or police officer can come to confirm the death. The body would then be taken to the morgue until further instructions.

If the person died by homicide, accident or suicide, the police will need to be called first.

How do I prepare for an anticipated death at home?

According to Marion McGuigan at Hospice Calgary, there is help for people who anticipate death, but do not want to die in an institution. Basically, she offers four pieces of advice: contact a Home Care nurse, contact a physician who is willing to make home visits, ask for help from your friends, and contact a funeral home.

Palliative Home Care personnel will work with you and provide ongoing family support and education. Marion told me that there are also physicians who will come to your home to provide care and support. "It's a myth that this doesn't happen anymore," she says.

It is important that the dying and the family find support outside the immediate family. This may be from your clergy and members of your religious group, from a bridge club, a quilting guild. Family members and patients do better when they have other support. There is less isolation and people are calmer.

"I encourage families to pick two or three funeral homes in their area and visit them while you have the time," she says. Alternatively, you might like to ask friends for a recommendation. You needn't make all the arrangements immediately, but may simply telephone and say that this person is dying and that you would like them to pick up the body when the time comes.

Finally, when death comes, the family may want to spend time saying good-bye. "I encourage people to do this," Marion says, "because after the body has been taken to the funeral home, things seem more formal and artificial. You can't hold them in quite the same way."

It may not be necessary to call the doctor at the time of death, since the death certificate could be signed at the funeral home. Remember, too, that if you call the funeral home to pick up the body in the middle of the night, it will take some time for them to get to you.

Discuss with the doctor and nurse the exact steps to be taken at the time of death.

When death occurs in a foreign country, what happens first?
This depends on whether or not you would like to have the body returned home, cremated before returning or disposed of in that country. A funeral home in your home town can help you make arrangements. You could also ask for help from your member of parliament or from your embassy or consulate.

Check your life, travel and medical insurance policy to see if there is help in transporting a body back to the country of origin.

What are the usual ceremonies around death?

There are three. A funeral is a ceremony held in the presence of the body or ashes soon after death. A memorial service or ceremony is held when there is no body present. It may be held any time after the death. A committal service is optional. It is usually brief, and may be in place of, or in addition to a funeral or memorial. Its purpose is to commit the body or the ashes back to the Earth. It is usually held at the crematorium, graveside or wherever the ashes are scattered or buried.

In addition, there is often a vigil, prayer service, wake or visitation.

People who belong to a organization, such as a fraternity or the armed services, might have additional ceremonies. Cultural and religious practices vary.

Other death ceremonies differ depending on cultural or religious practice. For example, within Judaism, the bereaved family sits shiva, which is a week of mourning after the funeral. During this week, friends visit the bereaved at home. In the Blackfoot First Nations tradition, burning sweet grass, praying after the ceremony and attending sweat lodge ceremonies for weeks or months is common. A giveaway ceremony (of the deceased's possessions) might also be held. Buddhists hold a memorial every seventh day for 49 days after the death.

What's the value of a ceremony?

Briefly, it helps us enter the transition of living without the person and to face the reality of the death. A father whose 23-year-old son disappeared said, "Closure is what we want. We want to find [his body] and put it to rest."

How do people decide between a memorial and a funeral service?

Religious and cultural traditions are the first consideration. Most people who do not believe in embalming (for example, Jews, Bahai's, Muslims,

Sikhs and Hindus) hold a funeral soon after the death. For Christians, atheists and humanists, the line is fuzzy. Many traditionally hold a funeral three days after death. If cremation is preferred, the time isn't important.

Francie Hagedorn is a Christian. When her father died suddenly in Calgary, Alberta, she says that one thing the family appreciated was the gift of time. "We decided on cremation, and this meant that we did not feel rushed. There was time for the family to gather from throughout the country; to hold each other, to grieve and to plan exactly what we wanted to say and do during the service. We had time to read some of Dad's journals and use some of his own words in the service."

What is the role of the funeral director?

Her or his role is to facilitate the event and provide goods and services such as facilities, preparing and transporting the body, provision of legal documents and permits, provision of vaults, coffins, urns, guest books, transportation and parking, ushering, names of clergy, musicians and so on. They are there to carry out your instructions.

How do I know which funeral home to choose?

Some people ask their clergy for a recommendation; some use the same one their friends and relatives have used before; some people look in the yellow pages and choose one at random. If you become a member of a memorial society, they will direct you before you need one.

When there were family funeral homes, this question was easier to answer. Families ran them, and served the families in the community. One home "looked after" your grandparents, parents, aunts, uncles. Now, families live apart from each other, and the family-run funeral homes compete with huge chains of funeral homes.

Funeral homes will provide a price list of their services and answer questions about goods, services and cost over the phone.

In Vancouver, British Columbia a new funeral service began in 1996. According to a *Maclean's* magazine article, Advantage Cremation and

Funeral Services operates out of a champagne-colored Ford Windstar van and offers savings of up to 60 percent. The funeral director will come to your home. The company is based in Houston, Texas, and is the largest funeral company in North America. In 1997, the company extended operations to Calgary, Alberta.

Must people always travel to a funeral director?

No. There is a Flying Funeral Directors of [North] America organization. Based in Minneapolis, Minnesota, pilots who are also funeral directors can fly bodies for autopsy from small centers to large, bring in caskets, and so on.

Where does the death certificate come from, and why do I need one?

The death certificate is a form from the government Department of Vital Statistics. It is filled out and filed with the provincial or territorial government by a funeral director. It costs in the neighborhood of $20. The funeral director can obtain copies for you which are necessary for the cemetery, airline refunds, life insurance, income tax purposes and other financial and legal transactions. The Widows Consultation Centre in Winnipeg, Manitoba recommends getting at least three copies. You can obtain additional copies from the Department of Vital Statistics.

When is an autopsy performed? Am I charged for it? How long does it take?

An autopsy may be ordered if the medical examiner cannot establish both the manner and the cause of death with reasonable certainty. In the case of a death of a child that might be a result of an accident, suicide, homicide or other unnatural cause, an autopsy is mandatory. If the death is part of a police investigation, an autopsy will be ordered.

The medical examiner does not need the family's permission to perform an autopsy. There is no charge to the family for an autopsy, but they have the right to request a copy of the report.

Usually the body is released for burial within a day or two after the autopsy.

Funerals

Why are some funerals so impersonal?
Sometimes it's because the funeral conductor didn't know the deceased.

Reverend Doug Cowan is a United Church minister in Calgary, Alberta. When I asked him this question, he told me about being called in to conduct a funeral for a woman he'd never met. When he visited the surviving adult sons, he asked them to tell him about their mother. The first brother said, "There isn't much to say." Doug turned hopefully to the other brother, who paused thoughtfully. Then he said, "I think my brother said it all." Okay. How would *you* conduct her funeral?

Are there discounts for people traveling to a funeral?
Yes. Most airlines have Compassionate Fares for close family members to attend a funeral. Ask your travel agent for details. Usually, you'll pay the regular fare at the time. Within 90 days, you'll apply for a partial refund, by filling out a form, providing a death certificate or funeral director's statement, your ticket and boarding passes.

What is the average cost of a funeral?
Sources vary, but the number I encountered most often was around $5,000. So much depends on personal choice. The casket is the big ticket item. Burial, cremation, headstones, honorariums and flowers cost extra.

What do I need to take to the funeral home?
Money is good. So is a friend. You will need a credit card or check as

a down payment. You need to know the maiden name of the deceased's mother. See Chapter 3 for more details.

If the body is going to be viewed, you will want to take clothes for the deceased. If the face has been damaged, you may be asked to bring a recent color photograph.

Why are most funerals held on a weekday?

Tradition, mostly, and because cemeteries charge extra to work weekends and holidays. This "extra" could be hundreds of dollars.

What is a pall?

It's a rectangular piece of fabric which is used to cover the casket. Covering a simple or elaborate casket can signify that we are all equal.

Burial

Is there any law against being buried in a shroud?

No. However, there may be cemetery rules that dictate you need a casket. Some also have rules that you must buy a grave liner or vault.

In this day and age, when people are more environmentally conscious and so on, why do most of us still bury our dead?

There are likely many answers to this, but one I liked was given by Dr. Laurie Pereles. She said that on a recent visit to Ireland she'd met three women whose friend had died. Regularly, the remaining friends packed up some cookies and a thermos of tea and trundled off to the cemetery for a nice visit at the grave site of their friend. (See also Chapter 7.)

Are all cemetery plots one occupant only?

No. Some allow double-decker interments in one grave, either bodies or ashes. You need to check.

Newer churches no longer seem to have graveyards. Why?
Most churches cannot afford the real estate.

Who owns cemeteries?
Municipalities, cities, religious institutions and private industry own and operate cemeteries and crematoriums.

How is the plot chosen? How much do they cost?
Families choose them at the time of death or long before. If you request it, funeral directors will assist you with this, and they will add their cost to your invoice. Each cemetery has a little map or blueprint showing available sites. The prices I found ranged from $125 to $1,700. The cost of city-owned plots with an upright marker in Calgary, Alberta rose in 1996 from $750 to $922. Maintenance costs are included in this figure. In comparison, a plot to inter cremated remains could cost less than $200.

How is the headstone chosen?
Some cemeteries, such as the Lakeview Cemetery in Yellowknife, NWT, allow people to create their own markers. There are large rocks pulled from Great Slave Lake and homemade metal boxing gloves; a pick axe and shovel crossed over a cement slab marks the grave of a miner. There are other creative expressions of love, as well as traditional markers.

Some cemeteries have specific guidelines about what type of headstone is permissible. After the service and cremation of her son's body, a woman decided to buy a headstone, then contacted the cemetery about installation. She was told that the type of headstone she had chosen was not permitted in their cemetery. (Indeed, some cemeteries will allow only monuments purchased through them.)

Most people buy a marble marker and have it engraved. These can cost anywhere from $2,500 to $40,000. A flat bronze marker can cost between $200 and $1,400.

What are burial vaults and when are they necessary?
A burial vault is a concrete, metal, or fiberglass container into which the casket is placed. Its purpose, I was told, is to "protect the casket." Vaults save the grounds keepers from having to refill the area above the casket when it collapses. You should check with the cemetery (or ask the funeral director) to find out if a vault is required. They cost extra.

Embalming

What is embalming?
Embalming is substituting a chemical fluid for the blood to temporarily preserve the body.

Is it required by law in North America?
No. Embalming is not required except in certain cases, such as transporting a body by public carrier, or when it will be longer than 72 hours before disposal of the body.

Do funeral homes recommend embalming, and why?
The funeral directors I spoke with did recommend it. They said handling an embalmed body is more sanitary.

How long does embalming last?
Considering that the Federal Trade Commission in Washington, D.C., prohibits funeral providers from making claims about embalming indefinitely, and that funeral directors when asked said they didn't know, it seems that preservation lasts long enough to have the body buried and that's it.

Is the family's permission required to embalm?
To put on make-up?

Yes, but the permission may be assumed. If you do not want embalming or make-up, you should say this clearly.

What are my options if I do not want the body embalmed?

Refrigeration of the body will preserve it, of course. The other option is fast disposal, such as having the body taken from the place of death to the crematorium.

Will embalming make the body look different if the funeral takes place three or four days after death?

Embalming apparently makes the skin dry and leathery. But since most of us don't see too many dead people, it's hard to judge whether it is embalming or death that makes the difference.

Are most bodies embalmed before cremation?

They are often embalmed if there will be a "viewing" of the body, and if it's religiously and culturally acceptable to the family. However, many people do not embalm before cremation.

When did embalming become common in North America?

Embalming was first practiced during the American Civil War. It came into more common practice in the early years of this century.

Coffins and Urns

Are there any rules about how the casket is built?
Is a homemade one OK?

Homemade is all right, but it needs to be durable enough to be moved. It would be a good idea to discuss this with the funeral director. Some funeral directors will ask you to sign a waiver in case the casket comes apart. In Quebec, funeral homes have the legal right to refuse your casket.

One funeral director told me that the son-in-law of a man who died built a casket for him. Because the man had been an amateur boxer, and because he'd loved gardening, he carved boxing gloves and flowers on the top of the casket. I also learned about some friends creating a coffin that was a work of art. It was presented to the dying person and she kept it in her living room as part of the furniture.

In their book *Lights of Passage*, authors Wall and Ferguson tell about a small American congregation having adopted the practice of building simple pine caskets for the deceased members of the church.

My sister told me about a company in Saskatoon, Saskatchewan that makes log caskets. They are popular with cowboys and outdoors people.

Is it possible to buy a casket wholesale?

No-frills casket companies are popping up in the 1990s. Nine companies opened in southern Ontario within three years. They sell direct to the customer at reduced prices.

Is there another alternative to a fancy casket without feeling cheap?

Some traditions cover the coffin with a pall (a rectangle of fabric), so expensive or cheap, everyone is equal. I understand that some families cover or drape the coffin with fabric they bring from home.

Do people make their own urns, too?

Yes. Sometimes they visit a showroom to get an idea of the size, then make their own box or make one from pottery. After all, it's just a big jar or box with a lid.

Is a coffin necessary if the body is to be cremated?

No. It is possible to rent a coffin for a funeral, and then have the body cremated in a cremation container. (A container is an inexpensive box that may be made of pressboard, cardboard, unfinished wood or canvas.) Crematorium personnel told me that they use a cremation container (rather than simply burning the body) out of respect for the dead. I suppose it's less awkward to handle a container, too.

I saw one in a funeral home, resting on the floor and more or less hidden from the snazzy coffins up front. It was a plain plywood container with yellow plastic "rope" handles. It sold for $195. There was no lining in it, or stain on the wood. It looked like a large homemade tool box.

What is the range of coffins offered for sale?

The range of coffins offered for sale is astonishing. You can even buy them waterproofed with spring mattresses. Linings can be satin or silk, and often have little tufted pillows like the ones on your old auntie's sofa, only white. Coffins are usually made of wood or metal. There are many different kinds and classes of wood and hardware adornment. It is possible to pay anywhere from $395 to $20,000 for a coffin.

A relatively new addition to fancy coffins is the "memory drawer." This is a little drawer in the side of the coffin, or in the lid, into which people can place letters, mementos, keepsakes, anything the family would like to bury with their loved one. It sounds rather Egyptian, doesn't it?

What does the display room look like?

This is often a large room where the opened coffins are displayed in rows on display stands. Depending on the mental image you have when you enter one, you may be pleasantly surprised that it doesn't look dark and dank, or you may be shocked.

According to one woman, it was an affront to be faced with a brightly lit show room, and she was unprepared for the finery presented. "There were lights shining on them. I wasn't prepared for a casket show room. Why don't they just have a catalog? Why don't they have simple choices that are not aesthetically repugnant but are not costly? Everything we looked at in a decent price range looked cheap and ugly."

There may also be a sample vault, and there will likely be various shapes and sizes of urns for cremated remains.

The Body

Who washes and dresses the body?

Usually the funeral director washes and dresses the body in clothing you bring from home. Some bereaved don't want to do it; others don't realize it's an option. In *A Treasury of Celebrations*, Virginia McConnell of Colorado wrote:

"My husband died very suddenly. When our family went to the mortuary, I asked for a pan of water and a cloth to bathe my husband's body before cremation. I had just read about an ancient rite where the person nearest to the deceased bathes the body, a custom that is still practiced in many cultures. Although we had never had this kind of experience before, it felt right. It was an important part of a grieving and healing process for me and a very special way to say good-bye."

People of the Sikh faith (and some others) traditionally go to the funeral home and pray as they wash and dress the deceased.

When I asked a funeral director why he didn't present this as an option to families, he said that it might put them on the spot and make them feel bad if they did not want to do it. If you would like to do it, discuss it with the funeral director.

Why are dead men dressed in suits?

Tradition. Today, people are becoming less concerned about this. If someone always wore jeans and a sweat shirt, there is no reason not to bury him in them.

Of course, not all dead men wear suits, anyway. In Orthodox Jewish tradition, for example, the body is dressed in a white shroud. All shrouds look alike, meaning we are all equal in death. Eastern Orthodox priests are buried in their vestments.

There was a time during the 1930s, my dad told me, that funeral directors sold "funeral suits." These were partial suits (front and sleeves) so that the deceased would look pretty swanky for his last public appearance, even though he may never have owned a suit in life. They cost $5.

During the 1960s, according to Jessica Mitford's book, *An American Way of Death*, funeral homes sold all sorts of funeral finery, including fine leather shoes for the deceased.

Why do some people "view the body"?

Mostly, this is tradition within the family or religion, which helps people understand that death has actually occurred (intellectually, we may understand, but emotionally, we still deny). After her grandmother's death, Leah Ann Lymer of Edmonton, Alberta said, "Our family went to view the body the night before the funeral. The minister encouraged us to tell our favorite stories about Grandma. At first we couldn't get the words out, but before long we couldn't stop talking. After we shared our memories, I could hardly take my eyes off my grandmother. By the time the funeral came, I had accepted that she was gone, but that I have at least 25 years of memories that are mine to keep. I think now that open caskets are not such a horrifying thing after all..."

Reverend Audrey Kaldestad of Westlock, Alberta says she finds it helpful to view the body. "It's so incredibly clear that the person doesn't live there anymore. The breath/spirit/ruach has left. [It] makes denial of death impossible. Now the task is to get used to it and go on in a new and different way—to build a new life."

Reverend Clint Mooney told me this story from Nova Scotia:

A man drowned in a faraway place and his body was not recovered for two weeks. When it was found and returned to his home town, the coffin had been sealed. No one ever saw the body. There was a funeral, a burial and a headstone was erected. "The woman had a difficult time believing that her son had died," Clint said. "On days when she believed that her son was dead, she would go to the cemetery and place some thing on his grave – a letter, a flower, something. But then weeks would pass when she would not go. Those times, she seemed to believe that they'd made a mistake. That her son was alive and would arrive home any minute."

What if some family members want to view the body, and others do not?

It is important to discuss this honestly before the funeral. After her mother's funeral, Anne Davies of Courtney, British Columbia recalled, "Dad didn't want the casket to be open, but my sister did. After the church service, they opened the casket for my sister with warnings that Mom had not been 'prepared'. Anyway, she was Mom, but she was frozen."

In cooperation with the funeral home, this situation can be handled. The body may be prepared for viewing and then a plain white sheet placed over it. When the whole family is together, the body is therefore concealed. If one or two want to view the body for a final good-bye, the others leave the room, and the sheet is drawn back. For the actual funeral, the casket can be closed.

Who places the obituary? Who writes it?

The funeral director will help you write the obituary and will ensure it is placed in the newspaper. The newspaper will bill the funeral director, and this will be added to their "services."

Alternatively, you can deal with the newspaper yourself. See also Chapter 4.

Cremation

What is cremation?

Cremation is incineration of a body. The temperature is between 1400 and 2100° F. It takes two or three hours.

Why do people do it?

Tradition is one reason. Today, more people are beginning to see it as an option considering that cemetery space is at a premium, burials are expensive and as my mother says, "a waste of trees."

Cremation, some argue, is more ecologically sound because of the amount of land required for cemeteries. Also, the cost of cremation is less than for a burial. Burial distressed one of my friends because there was water at the bottom of the grave into which her mother's casket was being lowered.

On the other hand, cremation may be unappealing to some. Children may be frightened by the idea of fire. It may be the abruptness of the destruction of the body that bothers them. Being returned to Earth in a slow, natural progression of change may be more satisfying.

In the end, cremation or burial is a very personal choice, influenced by tradition, culture and family. Arguing about it at the time of death is horrendous. It needs to be discussed before death.

How long do you wait between the cremation and the pickup of the ashes? How will they be presented to you?

It takes about a day between the cremation and the pickup of the remains. Unless you have taken an urn to the crematorium, they will be presented to you in a plastic or cardboard box.

**How do you know if the ashes you receive are the right ones?
Do you get them all? Are there crematorium inspectors?**

The answer to the first two questions is that you hope you get all of the
right ones. Yes, there are regulatory boards who inspect crematoriums
and listen to complaints about them.

Is there anything I need to tell crematorium personnel?

Yes. Tell them if the deceased had a pacemaker. These explode in
extreme heat. It would be good to mention any mechanical implant or
prothesis, too.

What do the ashes look like?

They are various shapes and sizes of charred bone and ash. The
crematorium pulverizes them before they are delivered to you.

**Are there rules about disposal of the ashes?
With whom do you check?**

Yes, there are rules about disposal in public places. Many people don't
know this, or choose to ignore it. You can check with the Department
of the Environment or the Department of Parks and Recreation (!).

What do people do with the ashes?

The answer is that people use their imaginations. Although they
sometimes unwittingly break the law, they spread them over lakes, in
parks, in forests, in gardens. They keep them for years in trunks, on
shelves, in suitcases. They travel with them. They bury them in an
urn. Sometimes they are placed in a crypt at the crematorium or
cemetery.

Some churches have a small "memorial garden" in the yard where
the minister will perform a committal service and place the ashes
under the sod of special area of the lawn. There may or may not be a
marker.

Other churches have a special memory wall where the ashes can be placed (rather like mail boxes at the post office) and sealed. The name of the person is on the outside of the wall.

According to the Manitoba Memorial Society, some people bury them in the cemetery plot of a relative (with permission) or on their property.

Many place them in a niche in a columbarium. Columbaria are usually located within a cemetery and could be a wall, a room or a whole building. Some funeral homes have indoor columbaria or "memory walls."

According to an article about funeral practices in *The Toronto Star* (August 14, 1994), Hindus usually try to arrange to have the cremated remains taken back to India to be scattered in the River Ganges.

The strangest tale I ever heard about ashes, though, is that a woman had her husband's placed in a large egg timer. Consider the implications of that!

Is it a good idea to spread the ashes from a small aircraft?
This sounds romantic, but unless you know what you're doing, it isn't. During my years in the North, I heard more than one story about someone holding the container out the window and having the ashes fly back in and swirl around the plane.

Body Bequeathal

How do I arrange to donate my body to medical science?
You can contact your nearest university and ask them to send you forms and information about this. You will fill out one form and return it to the institution. The other forms are for the time of death. You need to discuss this desire with your family. For more information, see Chapter 7.

Memorial Societies

What is a memorial society, and where do I find one?
Memorial societies have been established to help members obtain a
simple, dignified funeral or memorial ceremony at low cost.

It is a collection of individuals who pay a fee to join, and then are
assisted in making arrangements for their own death. It works more or
less like a co-op, and provides information about body donation, saving
money, burial, cremation, funeral planning and so on. The society's
purpose is to negotiate economically with the funeral industry and
provide information to the public and its members. It can also act as a
buffer between the bereaved and the industry. Since members have
filed their wishes with the society, funeral home, family, and perhaps
clergy, the family is relieved of the panic and expense of arranging the
ceremony "on the spot."

There are about 180 memorial societies throughout North America,
and if you move, membership is transferable. (See the Appendix for
addresses.)

**If funeral homes give the same service for less cost,
why would they want a contract with a memorial society?**
According to the Calgary Co-operative Memorial Society, it's numbers.
The representative told me that "Funeral homes are in competition
with each other. To have a contract with a memorial society means all
our members will use them. We have more than 8,000 members." Like
bulk buying, I guess.

PreNeed Funeral Plans

What is a PreNeed plan?

PreNeed plans simply accept your money in monthly installments while you're alive, to pay for the funeral after you are dead. It should not be confused with memorial societies.

Is a PreNeed plan a good idea?

According to information on the Internet (from KOCO-TV in Oklahoma City), people should ask questions when considering this idea: How will my funds be invested? What happens to the interest earned? Can I get a refund if I cancel? Can I transfer the plan if I move? What happens if the funeral home goes bankrupt, or if I die before the plan is paid in full?

There are options to PreNeed plans: join a memorial society or do your own planning with your family and set money aside in a trust or bank account to pay for it.

Mourning

Why do people mourn?

We need mourning times, I think, to be healthy individuals and healthy communities. Certainly we don't want to wear sackcloth and ashes all the time, but I think there's a place for them. Unless we take time to consider our losses and readjust to life, how can we fully embrace the joy of being alive, since death is part of life?

As a Christian, I would find the joy of Easter morning empty and meaningless unless I had taken time out for observance of Good Friday.

How long does it last?

There's no easy answer to this. Sometimes, forever. Within different religious and ethnic traditions there are set times for mourning. According to an article in *The Toronto Star* (August 14, 1994), there are formal grieving times for Sikhs (13 days), Muslims (40 days) and Jews (7 days). In the "olden days" in Canadian society, it was generally more defined, too. People wore black or a black armband and hung a special funeral wreath on the door. Some still practice this, but our society seems to be uncomfortable with it – and with tears, mention of the deceased, or yelling, for that matter.

THREE

A FUNERAL HOME – OR NOT

We heartily agree with funeral directors that death ceremonies, wisely planned, are important in meeting the social and emotional needs of survivors... We would add, however, that the amount of money spent has little to do with how well they meet those needs.
Author Ernest Morgan in *Dealing Creatively with Death*

This chapter walks you through what happens when you go to a typical urban funeral home. There are also stories about making arrangements without a funeral home, and buying limited services from one.

Using a Funeral Home

When you have decided to use a funeral home, you will phone to make an appointment. (You may wish to ask a friend to do this.) You will tell them where the body is and whether you want it taken to their funeral home or directly to a crematorium.

Ask precisely what you will need to take to your appointment in the way of information. You will need to know the deceased's birth date and place, usual and legal names, the names of the deceased's parents (including maiden name of the mother), and type of work that employed the deceased. You will need a check or credit card in order to leave a deposit. If finances are a problem, the director will discuss payment options with you, and has information about financial help from social services, the armed services (if the deceased was a veteran) and the federal government pension plan. When you go to your appointment, take a friend with you.

When I drove into a Calgary funeral home parking lot one brisk December morning, I saw a small snowplow at work, and six men wearing spiffy white shirts, suits and ties efficiently clearing with snow shovels. It was quite a merry and unusual sight. Formal-looking, you might say. There were to be five funerals there before the day was done.

As at most city funeral homes, the entrance is sparkling clean, the decor is hushed greys and pinks, there are vases of flowers, paintings of scenery, comfortable furniture and soft music to greet you. Bowls of candy (Life Savers in one place, I noted!) are displayed conveniently near boxes of tissues.

You will be led into a quiet "consultation room" where there are more candy and tissues. Catalogs for monuments, service folders or programs and flower arrangements are discreetly available. This is where you meet the funeral director and discuss your wishes. This is where you ask and answer questions. Forms to be completed include registration of death, permission to cremate, cemetery authorization, and obituary. You will likely be offered coffee or tea, and it will likely be served in bone china teacups.

This is where you will make decisions about:
- where you want the ceremony held
- whether you prefer cremation or burial
- whether you will provide a casket or urn or purchase one from them
- whether you prefer open or closed casket during the ceremony
- whether you want cremation before or after the ceremony, and whether you want the urn on display during the ceremony
- whether or not there will be a "viewing" of the deceased.
- when you will bring clothing for the deceased, and what to bring
- whether or not you want embalming
- whether you want to prepare the body yourself or have them do it
- whether you want to hire hearses and other transportation
- whether you want help in choosing a cemetery plot and/or monument or marker
- whether you want them to help you write and/or place the obituary in the newspaper
- whether you will contact your clergy or facilitator or want help doing that
- whether you want a stand or table to display photographs or other

personal mementos and where you want flowers, photos and so on, displayed

- whether or not you want a service brochure, what kind and what you want written inside
- whether or not you want them to help you find musicians, singers or taped music
- whether you want them to move the body or will arrange to do that yourself
- whether or not you want them to provide flowers
- whether or not you want them to hire caterers for you, and what you'd like served
- when you want the service of committal, and whether the funeral director will be involved

If you are asking them to help you make cemetery arrangements, you can also talk to them about your wishes and they can relay them for you. For example, some find it horrifying to see a pile of dirt beside the open grave and prefer it be covered with artificial grass. Others find artificial grass insulting. Some want to help fill the grave after the coffin is lowered and want spades available. So think through what you want to see or avoid seeing, tell the funeral director, and he or she will make it happen.

Eventually, you will visit a room where coffins are kept. It may be a shock to see them, so be prepared. They seemed huge to me, almost like cars. Many of them are polished to a shine of which any teenage car-owner would be proud. They come in a variety of metals and woods with white satiny fabric linings. Some are pretty frilly; it's hard to imagine a cowboy lying on these sheets. It all seems bewildering at first, because although we have all seen showrooms for cars, washing machines or computers, few of us have ever seen a room full of coffins. Take a deep breath before you enter the room. If the funeral director leads the way "somewhere," and you're not sure where you are going, ask before the door is opened.

The room is usually brightly lit, and if you are lucky, the prices will be prominently displayed. If you are not lucky, you will have to ask about each one, which means you can't look by yourself. If you are lucky, you will enter a room that has a wide range of prices. If you are unlucky, you will have to ask to see less costly versions. This is why it is a good idea to have an advocate with you. A friend who is slightly removed from the emotions you are feeling, can take notes and ask direct questions for you. They can question you too, about the purchase of this item which will run anywhere from $195 for a plain plywood box with rope handles (used during cremation), to the star-studded models that might cost $20,000. Many coffins are in the $3,000 to $5,000 range.

There are urns on display, too. Some look like a vase with a lid; others are a simple polished wooden box. Still others come in the form of hollow sculpture. (I will wonder now, when I enter someone's living room and see dolphins leaping over rocks or deer climbing a hill *who* exactly they are leaping or climbing over.) I saw one in the shape of a set of old golf clubs in a bag. I was also told about an urn in the shape of cowboy boots. Funeral director Dave Sellick said he knew one woman who did not want to pay $200 for a plain urn for her husband's remains. Instead, she went to a pet cemetery and bought basically the same thing for $50. "Her kids thought she was off the wall," Dave said, "but she didn't care."

You may also have the opportunity to purchase jewelry into which can be placed some of the ashes of the deceased. Funeral director Ernie Hagel explained that because families often live in different locations, this means that each member can have some of the ashes. For me, this gave new meaning to the phrase "scattering the ashes." In this case, it might mean Hong Kong, Yukon and Switzerland!

You will also likely be shown a "visitation room" which is a simple room with adjustable lighting. If you want the body of the deceased displayed in a casket prior to the ceremony so that people may pay their last respects, this is where it happens. It is up to you whether you want flowers or mementos there. Sometimes close family members will meet here for prayer and reflection time before the public ceremony. Near this room, there are often couches and chairs where the family can "take a break" away from the body to talk, collect their energy and have a cup of coffee.

Finally there is the room where the ceremony will take place. A lot of these look like churches, with pews, song books, organ and pulpit or lectern. Sometimes they have stained glass windows, too. Some of them have a curtained off "family room," with a washroom adjacent. Presumably this is where the family can hide their tears but watch the proceedings. Apparently, families don't use them as much now as they once did, preferring to be with everyone else, tears or no tears.

According to the Alberta Funeral Service Association, funeral home services offered include:

- removal from place of death
- obtaining medical certificate from the doctor
- completing government forms
- registering the death with the government
- obtaining necessary permits
- embalming, dressing and cosmetic restoration of the body
- preparing and placing death notices in the media
- arranging for and caring for flowers
- consultation with clergy and preparation of the clergy's record
- consultation with crematorium and/or cemetery
- disclosure of possible financial benefits available
- attendance and supervision at the service

In addition, you can rent their chapel, reception area and hearses. In the mid-1990s, the average cost for a traditional funeral was $5,000.

Recent Changes

Of the many changes that have occurred in the funeral industry in the past decade or so one is the amount of information they offer in the form of booklets and pamphlets about grief education, local workshops and seminars. These are displayed on tables throughout the public areas and in meeting rooms. They are near advertisements for monuments, but are worth looking at. Bereavement groups such as The Compassionate Friends, a group for bereaved parents and siblings, try to make their brochure available through funeral homes. Booklets also contain financial advice about widow's pension, federal pension, assistance for armed services veterans, crimes compensation board, workers compensation, and so on.

Some funeral homes have started holding annual memorial candlelight services for anyone who has lost a loved one throughout the year.

Annual memorial tree plantings are also coming into vogue. Each summer, trees are donated and each fall, families are invited to select a tree in memory of their loved one and attend a special dedication ceremony.

Your Choice

You may want to make all of the arrangements yourself. On the other hand, you may feel too overwhelmed, sad, or frenzied to be bothered driving to the newspaper office, the cemetery, the flower shop, or wherever, and simply want to leave the running around to someone else. You will pay for this, but you are at liberty to buy some services and refuse others. The best advice is to think ahead now. Do some planning, make some notes, visit a funeral home before you need to, and talk with your family. If you choose to hire a funeral director, take a friend with you.

Without a Funeral Home

Not everyone wants the involvement of a funeral home, even if one is available. Some hire a director, but only for limited services. Hutterites, for example, hire the director to embalm the body, but do all other preparation themselves, including laying out the body for viewing in his or her own bed. The members of the colony build the casket, conduct the funeral, dig the grave and close it.

Marilyn's Story

Marilyn Perkins selected her services carefully. She is a choir director in Calgary, Alberta. When Irma Perkins died at age 88, Marilyn and her brothers, Ken and Roger, did not hire a funeral director.

Marilyn says that her mother, who was ever practical as well as lots of fun, wanted an inexpensive memorial service, and that "I'd promised to do my best. Our one area of disagreement was over where her ashes would end up. Mother thought it would be too much trouble to have them interred with my father's in Toronto, whereas I was sure that we could manage it. (There is a plot here where my grandfather is buried, with a second plot available beside it. 'You could stick me in there,' Mother said. 'It does not really matter to me.') I think my brothers and I made the Toronto arrangement more for ourselves."

Irma died in hospital in the presence of her doctor and Marilyn. "This made it easy to get the death certificate signed," Marilyn says. "I made arrangements to transport Mother's body directly to the crematorium, and went there the next morning to present the death certificate and authorize cremation. I had to purchase a temporary urn ($20), cremation container ($140), pay the cremation fee ($260), and the professional services fee ($465). They provided an urn and arranged to have the ashes transported to the cemetery in Toronto." (The cost for transport to Toronto was $35. In 1996 the cost for all this came to $920.)

Marilyn and her brothers planned the memorial service in conjunction with the minister at the church where Irma had been a member. Friends offered help, and it was accepted. They functioned as ushers and greeters, donated a memorial book for people to sign and provided tea, coffee and refreshments at the reception, which was also held in the church.

Additional expenses included the obituary, which her brother wrote ($296), bulletin covers for the order of service ($11.50), and a caretaker's fee ($50). The family also made a donation to the church and gave honorariums to the organist and minister. In addition to music played by the organist, Ken played a violin solo.

The Toronto costs were $192 for the interment and $183 to engrave the marker that was already present on the plot where Marilyn's father was buried.

Following their mother's wishes, this family put together a beautiful, simple and dignified ceremony. Irma would be proud.

Marty's Story

Marty Brown is a journalist living in the Northwest Territories. Marty has been involved in "traditional" funerals in southern Ontario, and in funerals that were different from them in Fort Smith, Rankin Inlet and Yellowknife, Northwest Territories. "Generally speaking," she says, "the ceremonies seem more personal in the North." This could be partly because communities are small and there are no funeral homes; family and friends are more involved.

Marty recalls that the first northern funeral she attended was in the Anglican church in Yellowknife. It was for an artist who had frozen to death.

"Our sons were friends," she says. "I went for my son more than anyone. The body was at the front of the church in a plywood coffin made by a brother-in-law. The coffin was open showing his black lips and fingernails, and burn marks on his face, all the result of freezing. 'Odd,' I thought, my southern prejudices showing. 'Why have an open coffin so everyone sees how ugly death can be?' But then I thought, 'Why not? These are the facts. This is how it is. Why pretend?'

"After the service the coffin was loaded onto the back of a pickup truck for the trip to Hay River for burial, a distance of 600 kilometers. There are no fancy limousines in the North.

"When I was in Fort Smith, an old man was found dead behind the hospital. Heart attack. A few days later I was walking down the street and heard the cathedral bells ringing. (Fort Smith had hoped to be the capital of the Northwest Territories at one time. They built a huge cathedral suitable for the home town of the Catholic Archdiocese. But Yellowknife was chosen, and the Fort Smith population did not explode as planned; the cathedral lives on.)

"Out of the cathedral came the pallbearers, all wearing clean jeans, ball caps and sports jackets, carrying a fancy coffin, obviously sent up from the south. A black, freshly washed pickup truck backed up to the cathedral steps. In went the coffin, in went the pallbearers and all drove off to the cemetery.

"In Rankin Inlet, Inuit funerals often take place the day after death. The bodies are washed and dressed by local women. Coffins are made in the community. Services are held in churches or in the school gym.

"Death is a fact of life in the North. It's often not pretty, but people in the past have lived with starvation, accident and disease. Lately, there is suicide. It can be a violent land, with violent deaths. Death is not frightening. It stares you in the face daily."

Erica's Story

Erica Tesar is a teacher and writer. Her husband Don, died in a hunting accident near Yellowknife in January, 1990. The police came to her door to inform her. Don's body had been taken from the bush to the hospital.

The first thing Erica wanted to do was see Don, but she was not allowed at first, because the coroner had not finished the medical examination and report.

One of their daughters lived in England and did not have a phone. It took perseverance to persuade British police to find her and inform her of her father's death and her mother's wish that she return home. Erica says, "I put everything on my husband's American Express credit card. How do you do it if you haven't a card yourself, or money? And how could I be in two, three, five places and hearts at one time?"

Erica finally was allowed to see her husband's body the next day, but requested a sheet be placed over him. "We had promised that we would not see each other dead and that no one else would. I had been brought up with death and will not look at someone who is not there, or has been to death's beauty parlor. So I sat alone with my darling, darling man and we talked. This was between 24 to 36 hours after he died... I kissed him through the sheet and then went to look at coffins.

"We don't have a funeral parlor in Yellowknife, [but a couple makes arrangements, sells coffins, and has one hearse for hire]. The coffins were in a basement garage. It was 36 degrees below zero. There were old tires around, and stuff, garage stuff. There were three choices – one was really ornate, another looked like a pauper's. We took the middle one. He'd have hated it, I know, and likely would have preferred the pauper's. A friend said he'd make one of pine. I wish I'd let him.

"I was swamped with people. They brought food, love and curiosity. I arranged a wake at home. We drank the last of Don's homemade wine and a keg of beer. More than 200 people came. We played Don's favorite music and visited. His [closed] coffin was in the living room surrounded by flowers and candles. We carved messages in the coffin cover, and the grandchildren decorated it with drawings and sticker angels. We stuffed messages and letters in through the crack."

Don's body was to be cremated, which meant a three-hour plane ride to Edmonton, a further medical examination on arrival, and hotel accommodation for Erica and the children.

"The plane left at 8:00 a.m. The hearse arrived at 7:00, and I realized we should have just loaded Don in the back of the suburban, but we didn't. I rode with Don and we had a farewell tour of the city with a police escort. The driver forgot we were going to the airport and turned in at the cemetery. We had to shoot the traffic lights to make the plane.

"People met us at the airport to say good-bye, including a bagpiper. I don't remember much except we stood there, the children and myself and there were lots of people expecting a prayer or a speech, but I couldn't speak. I didn't want him to go into that white foam container in the hold of the plane, but he did. I didn't want his body to leave Yellowknife."

In Edmonton, the family had a private time with Don's body, then a further medical exam was performed [because he was from out of province]. Two of the children returned to Yellowknife immediately, the others stayed with Erica overnight in order to pick up the remains.

"The box looked like a file index, plastic. I signed 'here, here, and here,' and paid them. I wrapped the box in sealskin and returned to the airport.

"I didn't want him to go through x-ray security, but a pompous woman said he had to. I argued that I'd rather walk and created quite a scene. I wish I'd hit her. I finally gave in only because the kids said I was hurting myself, but I wouldn't let them touch him."

Six months later, under the midnight sun, Erica says she finally said good-bye to Don properly at their place on their island. "It was just the two of us. I ate his ashes, I scattered them, I buried them. I put them in every nook and cranny. I kept some, took some to Belgium, where he was born, and some to England where his mother lives."

Convention and tradition are there for those who wish to follow them. But for some, circumstances or the heart take precedence.

FOUR

PLANNING A CEREMONY

I wish I had known what I was supposed to do.
I didn't know what we could say,
when we could speak, or what our role was.
Part of the problem was that Mom was a strong Catholic
and it seemed as if the church who had her faith also had the right to
bury her as one of their own.
Yet, she was also ours.
The church had all the ritual and all the rules,
and we had only our grief.
Anne Davies

I hope that you will have the opportunity to read this chapter and file it away in the back of your mind for future reference. This chapter is meant to guide you through some of the thinking and planning for whatever manner of ceremony or ritual you want to create, and to show how others go about creating a ceremony.

Whether or not you choose to involve a religious leader or funeral director in the ceremony, you should feel free to make suggestions and work with your immediate family and friends to decide what will happen.

Although it is possible for the people closest to the deceased to conduct the ceremony, there are three reasons people call others for help: to have someone who is clear-thinking and a little bit removed from the emotional turmoil; to have someone who has some experience and/or training who can make suggestions or present options that may not occur to you; and finally, they can act as an advocate for you in the event that you run into problems. Once in a while, for example, the coroner may say they need to keep the body for a more lengthy autopsy than you had anticipated. An advocate can jump the hoops with you.

The obvious reason for asking your religious leader for assistance is that you are religious, or the deceased was.

How Some People Do It

Bill Phipps is an ordained minister in the United Church of Canada. He estimates that he has conducted about 100 funerals and memorial services. I asked him how he does it. How does someone enter into one of the most personal events in the life of a family and be of help?

"You want the funeral to be authentic to the person who died and to the family that remains," he said. "I say the same thing to families as I say to couples planning their wedding: When people leave the ceremony, what is the major feeling that you want them to have? I also ask them to pay attention to memories that they would regret not mentioning sometime later." After initial contact, he asks them to think about four things for later discussion and planning: readings, the eulogy or personal tributes, symbols and music.

"Readings can be anything – scripture, poetry or other readings. Sometimes people find a newspaper clipping or a poem from a magazine that grandma carried in her purse for years. Obviously, it had meaning for her. That could be used.

"I ask them to name family members, friends or colleagues who would be willing to write a personal tribute. This makes more sense than having someone who didn't know the person deliver something irrelevant. I suggest that it be typed, and I assure them I will stand near them if they wish. If they cannot continue reading, I can take over. This seems to work well. If the person who died is older, it sometimes works out that three generations speak: child, grandchild and friend. Increasingly, people are relying less on the minister to do everything. I think this is good. If it isn't possible for anyone to deliver the tribute, I interview the family and ask them to tell me their stories."

Bill suggests that people bring photos and symbols of the life of the deceased – a computer, an apron, golf clubs, a guitar – whatever they think symbolizes the person. "People use words to remember the deceased, but visuals also help us. A symbol brings in the elements of life and gets away from the "other worldly" symbol of an urn or casket with flowers. It helps us focus our minds, and brings a personal touch to the occasion.

"I advise people not to sing hymns unless the people are a church family. It's pathetic to hear a few weak voices making an effort. On the other hand, if the people are accustomed to singing, it can be uplifting.

"People are easier now about laughter," he says. "I let people know that it's appropriate and all right. I think in general, funerals are becoming more real. People are more honest in what they say about the deceased, and laughter is sometimes okay.

"If the deceased and the family were not particularly religious, I wouldn't use a lot of religious language. If the family is religious, but the deceased was not, I might talk about how the religious faith can comfort, but I wouldn't lay it on the deceased. It has to be true to both the deceased and to the family. I don't preach a sermon. After someone delivers a personal tribute, I will put the tribute into a more general context, into God's larger scheme of things. For example, if one of the traits of the deceased was compassion, I encourage learning from that person. Our world needs more of it. I'd suggest that people let compassion live on through them. I don't believe that a funeral is the time to evangelize. It's an important time in the life of people. I hope they feel they've been treated with dignity and respect. I'm glad if they leave the church knowing that the church met them at their point of need. That's enough."

Betty Norris Rykes is a lay pastoral minister in Brandon, Manitoba. She also offers her experience in creating ceremonies.

"I try to be respectful of others," she says. "There may be people who are not at home in a church. When I introduce Scripture, I might preface it by explaining that the passage was written by someone pouring out their grief or their questions; that people have, for thousands of years asked the same questions we ask: Where is God? How do I pray?"

Betty says that she uses conversational language, not "church" language, "because that alienates people."

Although innovation is good, Betty says that when she's burying an older traditional person, she worries less about inclusive language or new theology than she does about comforting the bereaved. "If they want to sing 'The Old Rugged Cross,' then that's what we sing. My role is to facilitate anything happening that they want to happen. I'm there to facilitate the celebration of life and to help with the grieving."

Betty also makes it her business to find out if children will be present. If they will be, she suggests that someone be at the funeral specifically to be with them, and to answer their questions.

Reverend Catherine MacLean has served in congregations in New Brunswick, Northwest Territories and Alberta. She says people often tell her that they don't want a "funeral," they want a "celebration of life." "They seem to feel this might be innovative, that I'll be surprised when they say it. But I think, *of course* we're going to do that. No problem. There is an assumption that a funeral is not going to be a celebration of the person's life. When I suggest that we sing *Joyful, Joyful, We Adore Thee*, (which I think is a wonderful funeral hymn for someone for whom life has been good and death not painful or unexpected), sometimes there's a real surprise."

Catherine sounds a cautionary note when recalling some eulogies she has heard. "When others are going to speak at a funeral, I always ask them to do it before I speak. People will often tell a story and then do a little theologizing, such as, 'God was ready to take her home.' And that's the reason I put it first, so I can deal with that theology and say, 'No, I don't for a minute believe that God would cause you this pain by taking this person you love.'"

Although it's hard to tell at most funerals, not all of us are saying good-bye to a "loved one." Sometimes, the relationship has been terrible. I asked Catherine about her experience with this.

"One funeral I conducted was for an abusive man. There were five people at the service, including his wife. She received flowers and food and care, but people didn't feel they could say farewell to him, I guess. She was well supported, but not at the service. It was a real challenge.

"People used to say they hoped that when he drove down the road drunk that he'd crash and not reappear.

"I usually talk about the good things, the things the deceased has contributed to the world. In this case, there wasn't much. I tried to be really honest because I knew that she knew that I knew what he was like. There was no need to pretend.

"I talked more to and about her than I usually would have, and about what her life might be like now that she was alone. I talked about what she had given him. She was a musician, and he'd never approved. At his funeral, we had lots of music, for her."

Another of Catherine's funerals was for a hermit. "It wasn't a negative impression he'd made on the world, it was no impression. He'd just retreated from the world. Usually, I can talk to the family about missing the deceased. But his brother and sister didn't have a relationship with him when he was alive, so what could they miss? He'd rejected them and everyone else years ago and gone to live in the woods in New Brunswick. That was a really difficult one."

Later in this chapter you will read how two children dealt with the death of their abusive birth father.

Whether you conduct the ceremony yourself, or call in others to help you, you will create a flow of events, rituals and music.

A Sample Structure of a Ceremony

Welcome
Prayer
Music
Reading
Personal tribute(s) or eulogy
Statement, affirmation of life or sermon
Music
Reading
Benediction/closing
(Within Christian communities, Communion may be served.)

The Welcome

The welcome is usually given by the one who conducts or facilitates the funeral (rather like the mistress or master of ceremonies). In addition to the general welcome, you may wish to thank and name some particular people for attending, especially if they have traveled some distance. If you choose not to use an order of service (or program, bulletin or service folder), you may want to outline what will happen during the ceremony.

The welcome might also include an acknowledgment of grief shared by everyone, gratitude for support shown, and acknowledgment of the circumstances around the death.

The Prayer

The prayer is usually offered by the religious leader, and within various religions there are prescribed prayers spoken at the ceremony. Outside of formal religious ceremonies, or in religions that encourage discussion and participation, the prayer may have input from you.

The Readings

The readings can come from a variety of sources. In religious ceremonies, at least some of the readings are from Scripture. Psalms are often used. Other readings may be poetry, a short essay or a short piece which was favored or written by the deceased. It would be good to preface the reading with a word about why it was chosen for this particular person. At his mother's funeral, Terry Wyman of Calgary read *Badger's Parting Gifts,* a beautiful children's story by Susan Varley. Anne Davies of Courtenay, BC suggests that *Love You Forever* by Robert Munsch might be a good funeral reading, but I've never made it through that story without crying.

The Music

Music feeds our souls. During a ceremony, it can also provide respite from thinking and from words. Many of us can't absorb word upon word upon word. A music "break" gives us a little rest to mull over what has been said. It can allow tears that have been blocked, to flow. It can help us remember the deceased in the way that has more to do with emotion than with information. It can be a prayer.

Music performed at funerals is widely varied. Soloists who are "on call" at funeral homes will sing requested music. Church choirs and soloists, drummers, jazz bands, organists, bagpipes, and recorded country and pop have all provided music. In his book, *From Beginning to End: The Rituals of Our Lives,* Robert Fulghum relates the story of a jazz fan's graveside ceremony. This woman had planned her whole ceremony to take place at the cemetery. When the people gathered to bury her ashes, a traditional jazz band entered the cemetery playing her favorite piece in honor of her memory.

In Yellowknife, members of a classical quartet provided music for a fellow musician's memorial service. The three musicians played, and his chair sat empty but for his violin.

What I remember most about the traditional Black Baptist funeral for my music teacher in Toronto, is the music. It was uplifting, comforting, swinging, loud and wonderful. It lifted the roof off that little church. She would have loved it.

Two parents had written music for their son. Both songs were sung at the son's funeral. When Barbara Lewis' cousin died, she wrote and performed *Lullaby (for a deep sleep).* (You will find the words in Chapter 5.)

The whole congregation sang *Bless This House,* at the funeral of a woman who had sung it often during her lifetime. Cathy Lewis had made a recording of herself at the organ and given it as a gift to her parents. When Cathy died, her parents played that recording at her memorial service. At the ceremony for a man who loved organ music, and loved to whistle, his family arranged more music than words. The organist gave an uplifting recital. A pamphlet I picked up at one funeral home noted that at a service for a country music fan, the concluding taped music was Roy Rogers singing, *Happy Trails to You*!

Personal Tribute

The personal tribute or eulogy (eulogy means "good word") is likely the place you want to spend most energy. This may be delivered by a clergy person, facilitator, by you or by others who were close to the deceased. As suggested earlier, if you or someone closely related to the deceased decides to do this, it is a good idea to have the words typed clearly, so that if you cannot go on, someone else may finish the reading. There is no reason why more than one person cannot deliver personal tributes. In fact, this is a good idea if there are generations involved, or if the person's colleagues from work, school, the drop-in center or volunteer group would like to speak. (If more than one person speaks, it's a good idea to compare notes beforehand so there isn't too much repetition, and it's a good idea to set a time limit.)

I have attended some funerals which list the person's vital statistics and mention their work history and number of children. To me, that is sad. Although we could get carried away with placing the person on a pedestal, that isn't really the point, either. The personal tribute is meant to highlight the qualities of the person, (in effect, to bring the person "to life" again), to comfort the family, to inspire us, perhaps. What is it we can learn from this person's life?

At the funeral for Stan Harding of Calgary, there were many words spoken to honor his long and distinguished life and career, both by a colleague and by his son. But the words I remember most were spoken by his granddaughters. One told the story of feeling awful and having a broken shoe. She was just tiny. Her granddad sat down on the step to be with her and to fix her shoe. It was a touching and loving moment across the generations, and I felt happier knowing that story. Stories give meaning to our lives and to our memories.

Marian Hood is an Alberta teacher and poet. Her father died at age 68 in 1981. He had been a teacher and active within his church community. "Our relationship was always characterized by darkness and silence," she says. "We didn't hate each other; there was just a dark void between us for all of his life. Like many men of his generation bent by the experience of World War II, I think he was bewildered by the roles of husband and father, and his retreat was the church. My mother and I often did without him because he was on church business and there never seemed to be time left over for us."

At her father's funeral, Marian says she "came to learn that the man the minister knew and the man I knew as my father were very different. The minister said that he had seen a plane taking off shortly after sunrise that morning. As the plane banked into the sky, the light caught it, filling his eyes for a moment 'with sunlight and burnished gold.' He likened my father's life to that moment of light. I wondered how this could possibly be the same man I knew. I think the minister's words that day set me on a search for my father. The search isn't over yet, but I know more about him now and can accept those qualities in myself which were also his...

"It mattered tremendously to me that on the day of his memorial service the minister gave me the image of the plane to carry with me. It mattered that he knew my father better than, or perhaps differently than, I did."

So, the personal tribute can be whatever you need it to be. Generally speaking, it outlines the life of the person, and goes on to tell stories. As was mentioned earlier, humor is part of life, and as funerals are becoming more real, humor sometimes finds its way in, too. If the person who died had been fun-loving and humorous, it would be strange to omit that quality from the storytelling.

Sometimes the personal tribute can take a form other than words, or in addition to them. At one funeral for a young artist, his friends brought in some of his latest artistic creations and held them while the priest talked about them. At another, a slide presentation showed pictures of a young woman's life.

The Statement, Meditation or Sermon

A sermon or statement will be in the context of the faith tradition of the family and/or deceased. The beliefs about life and afterlife will likely be talked about, and are meant to comfort the bereaved. It is my feeling that this is not a time for evangelism, but rather a time to call upon the theological resources, the history and tradition of the faith to help put this particular life and death – and mourners' grief – into an overall context. You may want to ask your worship leader about what she or he will say, or ask them to include a particular faith story that is relevant and offers insight and comfort to you.

A statement, on the other hand, may simply be an affirmation of life without religious overtones.

The Closing

The closing or benediction will also likely be delivered by the funeral conductor, and again, you may wish to ask about it, have input into it, or write it yourself.

You or another may want to thank people for their attendance and to announce details about refreshments, the committal service (if there will be one), or that the deceased requested that the body be donated to medical research. If the deceased's organs have been donated, you might like to mention this, too.

The benediction can be as simple and gentle as, "The service has ended. Go in peace."

The Committal Ceremony

If the body is to be buried, there will be a gravesite ceremony of committal (that is, committing the body back to Earth). If you would like specific people with you, invite them. Do not assume that they will come, because many people skip this part. If you prefer to have this a private ceremony, say so.

The committal ceremony is generally brief, with a prayer, a short reading, and perhaps a symbolic sprinkling of earth.

This is an extremely emotional time. You need to make clear what you want to happen. For example, when you arrive, the casket will likely be placed above the opening in the ground. The funeral home or cemetery has a mechanical gizmo for gently and evenly lowering the casket. If you do not wish to see the casket lowered, tell them. If you would like it lowered, tell them that.

You may want to place flowers on the casket before or after it is lowered. Or, you may want to help to begin to close the grave. In times past, of course, this job was done by family and friends. Now, it is usually done by cemetery workers. Sometimes this is done symbolically by sprinkling earth on the casket; sometimes it is done with shovels.

My husband wanted to do this for his mother. For him and his sister, this meant closure. "It meant closing the circle," he says, "and completing the ceremony. It also meant physical hard work. I needed that; I needed more just than some more words." He asked the cemetery to make available several shovels at the grave site. When the ceremony had ended, the casket was lowered and family threw in shovelsful of earth. (Within Judaism, there is a tradition of using the backs of shovels for this, symbolizing that this task is not a hurried one.)

If cremation has been chosen, you have a number of options. You may want to accompany the body to the crematorium for a brief ceremony there. You may want to have the body taken there directly from the hospital. If so, tell the crematorium people you will pick up the remains at some later date and have a ceremony when you dispose of them.

There are several options open to you, principally because there is no hurry to do anything at all right away.

Some people, of course, keep the ashes at home. Others, I'm told, take them on the world cruise that was planned but didn't happen in time. Some bury them in a cemetery or place them in the churchyard by simply lifting the sod gently, and pouring them in. They may also be placed in a columbarium at the cemetery or crematorium. Some of these are outdoors, others are in buildings. There are also places in some churches especially for urns.

If you choose to scatter the cremated remains, you may turn to Chapter 2 for advice about this.

More Advice

If you anticipate that large numbers of people will attend, and you want them to sign a guest book, provide two books with removable sheets to avoid a long line-up. These can be incorporated into one book later.

Have a basket near the entrance for those wishing to put in sympathy cards. You may also provide small pieces of paper and pens for people wanting to write a message to the deceased. These can either be kept, burned or buried with the body.

Depending on the age, personality and desire of a child or teenager, consider some form of participation in the planning and ceremony. The reasoning behind inclusion is that if children are capable of love, they will mourn the loss, and the death rituals can help them do this. Adults, however, should explain what the child will see and hear during the ceremony. If the child decides to participate, (for example, by reading something), be prepared for a last minute change of mind. Lighting a candle, placing a symbol on a table or writing or drawing something for someone else to present, may be less stressful.

Other General Concerns

The other decisions you will need to make are:

- choosing a casket or urn
- whether or not the body will be present
- who will serve as pallbearers (Even if there has been a cremation, honorary pallbearers may be desired.)
- whether the casket is open or closed
- what photographs, symbols of life, and decor (flowers or not) are visible
- what to say in the obituary (which in some ways, serves as a public invitation to the ceremony, unless you say otherwise)
- whether to have ushers
- whether or not to have an order of service (which may include a photograph and some writing about the deceased)
- who will provide refreshments, and where they'll be served
- whether there will be a grave side or scattering ceremony (when it will be and who you want there)
- how children will be cared for

Choosing a Casket or Urn

The best advice I can give you about choosing a casket or urn, is to take an advocate with you. This may seem strange, but you need someone there to help make the right decision for you. When we are caught in grief and shock it is difficult make good decisions alone. Even other members of the family may not help, since they are in the same state as you.

It may be that you do want to spend thousands of dollars on a casket and vault and so on. But it may be that you are reacting to a stressful situation, and that under normal circumstances you would not choose to spend vast sums of money. There are so many different kinds of urns and a confusing myriad of caskets, that it takes a clear, calm mind to sort it all out. That is likely not you. Take a friend, your religious leader, or your neighbor to help you.

The Body

Whether or not the body will be present at the ceremony is your decision. If the deceased had wanted his or her body donated to medical science, and you agree, then there is no question. If you would like the body to be cremated, this can be done after the ceremony, or before. If you prefer burial, this usually happens after the ceremony.

If you would like to have the body at the ceremony, you will want to choose pallbearers. The usual number is six. Although in the past this was always done by men, today, women and men are serving. They are usually friends of the deceased. They accompany the body into the room where the ceremony will take place, and out to the hearse for transport to the cemetery, and from the hearse to the burial plot. If the funeral home is involved, there is usually very little actual carrying done, as the funeral home usually provides a rolling cart.

You will decide whether or not to have "a viewing" of the body in the days prior to the ceremony. In her book, *Questions and Answers on Death and Dying*, Elisabeth Kübler-Ross says that if the death follows a prolonged illness, where the family realized that they were losing their loved one, there is likely less need to "view" the body after death. I would add that if you have been with the person while she or he died, there is less need. But when the death is a complete shock, "it is important that the family view the body in order to face the reality of the beloved one's death."

Symbols, Photographs and Flowers

You may want to prepare a symbol or symbols to have on view during the ceremony and/or afterward. Many people use an enlarged photograph or a collage. A symbol may be anything from a guitar or a toy to a set of golf clubs. At the Montreal funeral for Winifred Holden – an actor in the film *A Company of Strangers* and a woman of many talents and friendships – her friends placed her scarlet rain hat, a photograph of her as a young woman, three toys she had knit, a picture she had painted, and the press book for the film on a table.

Symbols may also be something you'd like people to take home. A woman in Ontario planned her own funeral after learning that she had but months to live. She purchased several dozen flower bulbs to be distributed to friends at her funeral. Candles might also be distributed in memory of the light spread by the life of the deceased. Symbolically, each person is asked to carry that light forward.

Once, flowers were a huge part of the funeral setup. Mountains of them sometimes dwarfed the people. Fewer people have elaborate flower displays today, instead opting to have a few beautiful arrangements, and requesting that people donate to cancer research, a church, or some other struggling organization important to the deceased or family. Some people make their own simple arrangements by picking from their own gardens.

Instead of quantity, people are looking for meaning and symbolism in floral arrangements. Dried flower artist Marie Saretsky lives near Burr, Saskatchewan – wheat country. She says that people are asking about the meanings of colors and the meanings of the flowers themselves. She sees requests for wheat weavings and wheat wreaths, especially for farmers. Recently, Marie made a casket arrangement incorporating barbed wire and horse shoes for a rancher.

The Obituary

The obituary serves as a public notice to the world that your loved one has died. It might be seen as an invitation to the funeral – mentioning date, time and place of the ceremony. If you wish, your funeral director will help you to write it. Alternatively, you can contact the newspaper directly and either deliver or fax what you would like to say. There are no rules, particularly, but obituaries usually follow a format.

If you look in the newspaper today, you will see that there is an opening statement noting the person's name, place and date of death. Sometimes the survivors are listed, sometimes the predeceased are named as well. A short recap of the person's life and interests is included, followed by the address, date and time of the ceremony. Finally, the family often thanks special people, and requests that "in lieu of flowers, donations may be sent to..." The name and address of a foundation or charity follows.

The advantage to giving the obituary to the funeral home is that they receive a small discount from the newspaper, which is passed on to you. The obituary bill will show up on your bill from the funeral home.

When you decide to place the ad yourself, you need to know two things. First, the newspaper is not allowed to run an obituary without checking that the person has indeed died. Therefore, you will have to give them the name of your funeral director or clergy, or they will have to call the coroner to confirm.

Secondly, you should know that if you run the obituary in a small town newspaper and in a large city newspaper, you will be charged different rates. Newspapers charge per agate line (1 inch equals 14 agate lines – even in metric Canada). The charge per agate line is based on the circulation of the newspaper. In a large circulation paper, you may be paying $50 or more per inch. Also, if you decide to run the obituary for three days, for example, you can expect to pay a large sum for the first day, less for the second, and back up to the first sum on the third day.

You may choose to run a very short obituary simply stating the facts on one day, and a longer one on the second and third days.

There is no additional cost for a black and white photograph, other than adding more inches to the length of the column.

Service Folder

A service folder or program is optional. Some people simply announce what will happen next in the ceremony. Others see the order of service as another way to make a tribute to their loved one, and pour a lot of time, energy and creativity into making one. The funeral home has blank ones which they will have printed to your specifications. Likewise, the church likely has bulletin covers which you could use. They are also available at church supply stores. Some covers are very "religious" looking, and others are simple photographs of perhaps a tree, or lake scene, or a candle.

Alternatively, you may want to make your own, using a computer and the new photocopying technology available. A black and white or color photograph of the deceased can easily be reproduced on the cover. Inside, you may want to write a small tribute, print a poem, or place some other piece of writing, Scripture or a quote. On one page, you will print the order in which the proceedings will take place, with perhaps the names of people leading or contributing to the ceremony, hymn numbers, sources of readings or other music, and so on. You and your family may also use this as a place to thank people specifically or in general for any kindnesses received. You may also want to include the address of any organization to which you'd like donations sent.

Refreshments

The purpose of this time is for the bereaved to receive support from their community. It took a few funerals for me to figure this out. I thought it was to eat.

This is a time for people to greet one another and to greet you. It can be an emotionally draining time but it can also be very supportive seeing old friends who care about you. Lindy Jones offers this advice from her experience: "We spoke to and hugged every person who came through the receiving line. If you are up to it, it is good to be able to do this. People need to feel that they have said something. Later, when they pass you in the grocery store, they may not know whether it is the right time to speak or know what to say. At the funeral, all they need to do is hug you. Hugging in the local Safeway may not always seem appropriate."

You do not want to be worried if the coffee runs out. You will need all your energy focused on the people present. Traditionally, the "church ladies" catered to funerals, providing tea, coffee, juice, sandwiches and squares. This cannot be taken for granted anymore, since many women are working outside the home.

Sometimes a caterer is hired to do this. Other times, friends ask what they can do to help – I would take them at their word and ask them to help take care of refreshments for you. They may round up their friends who also would be glad of some way to help you.

Refreshments are sometimes served at the family home after the ceremony and the burial. Sometimes they are served wherever the funeral takes place, after the funeral but before the committal (if there is to be one).

There are no rules, except that the time and place be convenient and simple, and that you receive support from people who love you.

Alternative Memorial Ceremonies

Imagine:

Your friend dies in a distant place and you cannot attend the ceremony.

Your father died ten years ago, and your mother arranged a funeral that was unsatisfactory. Their religion was not yours. It's bothered you ever since.

Your father abused you when you were a child. He has died now, and had a "regular" funeral. All you could do was stay away.

When you were young you had an abortion. You think about that periodically and wish you could find some closure.

When you were working in a home for disabled adults, a young man died. The funeral was quick and absolutely impersonal. It seemed like his life wasn't worth much. It still makes you mad, even 20 years later.

You were adopted when you were six years old. You saw your birth father a few times a year for the next few years. One day, you hear that he's dead. The funeral is over. You want to do something.

All of these situations are real. All of them left a legacy of frustration or sorrow wanting closure. Although we occasionally spend some time and energy thinking ahead about the financial costs associated with funerals, we seldom talk about the emotional costs. When it comes to death, the cost of "unfinished business" can be very high. It sounds simple to look after our emotional needs, but many of us are conditioned by society or family or our own high expectations of ourselves that we can neglect to do it. Many of us want to keep a stiff upper lip, to be strong and brave. In our collective memory, we carry the image of Jackie standing straight and brave after President Kennedy was shot. But all we saw was a picture.

Taking time to mourn can help us live more fully today.

At a Distance

When my husband's mentor and friend Katharine Hockin died in Toronto, we were living in Edmonton and he could not attend. He contacted Katharine's family in Toronto and told them he would be "with" them at the same time and day that they gathered for the main celebration of her life. Before the funeral, the minister in Toronto announced that we were meeting in Edmonton simultaneously.

Our small western group gathered in a church meeting room. Someone brought a large white candle which we placed in the center of our circle. We prayed together, and gave thanks for her life. And then we told stories. People had brought photos, letters and newspaper clippings. My husband brought a stole that Katharine had crocheted at one of the millions of meetings she had attended in her life. For a time, we sat in silence. We talked about the people meeting in Toronto. And then we ended with another prayer. It was simple and good.

If you are planning a ritual of remembrance for someone you love, you may want to follow the outline for the ceremony at the beginning of this chapter, or use something similar to the following ritual.

Ritual of Remembrance

Hold this ceremony in any place that is comfortable or meaningful for you: your front room, a mountaintop, a field, a riverbank, or your backyard. Arrange chairs, blankets or cushions in a circle. Display one or more photographs, and some symbols of the person's life. Have on hand enough tapers for everyone. Set a large white candle in the center of the circle.

Ahead of time, photocopy the litany for each person.

Welcome
Light the candle.
Prayer: for courage and thanks for love among the people gathered.
Reading: Psalm 130
Reflections: about the person and his or her life.
Storytelling: by the people, in which they relate one story about why they are thankful to have known the person, or relating something they learned from the person.

Music: "Turn, Turn, Turn" by Pete Seeger
Reading: The Beatitudes (Matthew 5:3-10)
Reading:
Do not stand at my grave and weep;
I am not there. I do not sleep.
I am a thousand winds that blow,
I am the diamond glints on snow.
I am the sunlight on ripened grain.
I am the gentle autumn's rain.
When you awaken in the morning's hush;
I am the swift uplifting rush
Of quiet birds in circled flight.
I am the soft stars that shine at night.
Do not stand at my grave and cry;
I am not there. I did not die.
        – anonymous

Alternative Reading:
When I must leave you for a little while
Please do not grieve and shed wild tears
And hug your sorrow to you through the years
But start out bravely with a gallant smile;
And for my sake and in my name

Live on and do all things the same.
Feed not your loneliness on empty days,
But fill each waking hour in useful ways,
Reach out your hand in comfort and in cheer
And I in turn will comfort you and hold you near.

– anonymous

Ritual of Light: *(Candles are distributed to everyone.)*
Our light burns brightly but a short time. We give thanks for the light that glowed in (name). By our knowing (name), may we pass on the goodness that was embodied in (him/her).

Light your taper from the candle in the center of the circle. The light is passed around the group, one to the other. When all candles are lit, read the litany together.

Litany:

One: We gather to say farewell.
All: We remember (name) with love and tenderness.

One: We gather to say we will not forget.
All: We remember (name) with stories and silent recollections.

One: We gather to say farewell.
All: We gather to say we need each other.

One: We gather to pledge we will support each other in the months and years ahead.
All: In supporting one another, we add love to the world, in (name's) memory.

One: May we go from this place strengthened and supported. Amen.

Closing or Benediction: The ceremony has ended. Go in peace.

When the Relationship Was a Bad One

(The names are fictitious, but the story is true.)

Barry and his twin sister Anne had seen too much violence and upheaval by the time they were ready for kindergarten. They had learned that home is not a safe place. They had learned that home isn't for keeps, either, and that you might have to move to nine different foster homes in five years. Finally, you might get adoptive parents who say they'll keep you no matter what.

Living in their adoptive home, the twins periodically heard from their birth father. But one day, he went to jail after being charged for armed robbery. He died there of a heroin overdose. The children learned about his death after the funeral. The news began eight months of therapeutic intervention and patience and anger and love.

At the end of eight months, the children and their adoptive parents discussed the possibility of a ritual to mark their father's life and death. Barry's adoptive mother, Mary, says "For Barry it was a major process to work through his feelings about the death...the ritual marked the closure of this process."

With the help of a minister friend, Karen, the ritual was discussed and planned. Karen asked the children for suggestions about what they might like to do. Barry said he wanted to read the story of David and Goliath from the Bible.

Mary recalls that Karen then asked the children to make a list of both good and bad things they had lost in the death of their birth dad, recognizing that some, in the death of this violent and abusive man, would not be missed much. "Barry made his list 'invisible' but said his dad would know what was on it. One thing he did say was that he was sorry his dad never had a chance to fix himself and they never had a chance to be friends."

It was an informal ceremony. Karen talked with the children and said a short prayer. Each child had an opportunity to talk about what they had written. The papers were then burned, followed by the burning of sweet grass as a sign of healing, cleansing and letting go. (This ritual is part of the children's Native heritage and one with which the children were familiar.)

"Barry then read David and Goliath, from a Bible storybook which he had long treasured," Mary says. "He prefaced the story by saying that the reason it was important was because it showed God didn't always choose the big tough guys to do God's work. Sometimes little kids were important. (The story behind this was that Barry had on one occasion tried to stop his dad from beating his mother. Unlike David, he did not prevail against this giant.) We closed with another prayer, and then went to visit the grave.

"In many ways the biggest part of the ritual was getting there – the preparation the children did in order even to reach the point of being able to acknowledge the death and move on, the preparation and discussion of what we would do, and the walk through the cemetery to the grave site. I remember Barry walked both ways alone, at some distance from the rest of us, and returned to the group very peaceful. We went for ice cream before returning home.

"It took a long time for Barry especially to be able to ritualize the event – that's the biggest learning for me out of all this, I think, that the ritual marked a point of letting go, and that it could not have happened at the time of the death itself."

Although this ritual was designed for specific children, it could certainly be adapted for any of us who find ourselves in a similar situation.

Ritual of Letting Go

Hold this ceremony in any place you feel comfortable. Arrange chairs, blankets or cushions in a circle and have some incense, matches and a large red candle in the center of the circle. Also place a large bowl with sand in its bottom in the center, and something that for you, symbolizes change (perhaps a butterfly or an egg). Have on hand enough small pieces of paper and pens for everyone. Ahead of time, photocopy the litany for each person.

The person(s) for whom this ceremony is held may feel great satisfaction in being able to break something as a symbol of breaking with the past. If this is so, you may want to provide some glass or rocks and a large garbage can. The sound can be therapeutic. Just take safety precautions.

Another alternative would be to incorporate planting into this ceremony. Listed feelings, or symbols or objects belonging to the deceased could be planted beneath the root ball of a tree.

Welcome the people
Light the candle.
Prayer: of thanks for support and love among the gathered.
Words: about the purpose of the gathering.
Reading: Psalm 61:1-5 and 8
Reflection: about the person who has died and/or situation that has ended.
The Breaking: (*If the person wants to smash glass or throw rocks into a large garbage can as a symbol of breaking free from the past, invite him or her to do this now.*)
Music: "Turn, Turn, Turn" by Pete Seeger
Distribute paper and pens to everyone.
Invitation: to everyone to take a few moments and write words or phrases about feelings they would like to leave behind.
Prayer before Burning:
Creator God, Crucible,
We offer you our pain, our rage, our frustration, our grief, knowing that your arms are wide enough, your shoulders strong enough, your heart big enough to carry them. Hold us close. Whisper encouragement into our hearts and minds. Transform these feelings into courage and hope!

Be with us as we transform ourselves into the people you would have us be, into people of compassion and love, courage and laughter. Amen!

Invite people to enter the circle, light their papers with the candle flame and burn them in the bowl. (Invite them to do this in silence or to speak as they do it.)

The Burning

Light the incense and allow it to burn in the bowl among the ashes of the paper. You may want to pass it around the circle.

Music: (taped, instrumental)

Distribute the litany and read it together.

One: We mourn the loss of what could have been. It's human nature.

All: We grieve our yesterdays.

One: We are fearful that yesterday will bind us today.

All: We worry about our tomorrows.

One: People have always known about change. We learn it from the seasons.

All: But sometimes it is hard to believe in change. We learn this from people.

One: Then may we turn to the trees for our learning.

All: And remember their lessons:
    seedlings grow among wild, windswept rocks in cold climates,
    nursery trees, even in death, give nourishment to new life
    and old stumps sprout anew in springtime.

One: We, too, can celebrate the promise of transformation

All: And ask for strength for its fulfillment in us.

One: With the help of the Creator who is ever creating,

All: And the help of people who love us, we step into the future.

One: We are not alone.

All: We are not alone. Thanks be to God. Amen.

Prayer: (for healing)
Closing: The ceremony has ended. Go in peace.

Worksheet for a Funeral or Memorial Ceremony

You may want to use one of the ceremonies directly from this book, create your own, or take bits and pieces from several sources.

Facilitator _____

Date and Time of Ceremony _____

Location _____

Prayers _____

Music _____

Eulogy _____

Meditation or Affirmation _____

Readings _____

Refreshments _____

Pallbearers _____

Closing _____

Service of Committal

Facilitator _____

Location _____

Date and Time _____

Special Guests _____

Notes _____

_____

_____

_____

o

FIVE

THE DEATH OF
A CHILD

Like most people, my wife and I had grown up with an image of God as an all-wise, all-powerful parent figure who would treat us as our earthly parents did, or even better. If we were obedient and deserving, He would reward us. If we got out of line, He would discipline us, reluctantly but firmly. He would protect us from being hurt or from hurting ourselves, and would see to it that we got what we deserved in life...

...Then came that day in the hospital when the doctor told us about Aaron and explained what progeria meant. It contradicted everything I had been taught. I could only repeat over and over again in my mind, "This can't be happening. It is not how the world is supposed to work." Tragedies like this were supposed to happen to selfish, dishonest people whom I, as a rabbi, would then try to comfort by assuring them of God's forgiving love. How could it be happening to me, to my son, if what I believed was true?
Harold Kushner, in *When Bad Things Happen to Good People*

Try as we might, we can rarely make sense of the death of a child. Parents are meant to be buried by their children, not the other way around. Bill Phipps of Calgary says, "The primary reason why the death of a child is so difficult, is that in our culture – unlike many other places in the world where children do die frequently – the death of a child in North America is unusual. It goes against everything we think is right, fair and natural. It assaults our senses. I think we're getting better at acknowledging this."

Pregnancy Loss

A surprising number of pregnancies end in miscarriage; some say the rate is as high as 25 percent. Although miscarriage occurs this often, and although abortion is routinely carried out, it does not mean that this loss is easy, nor should be unacknowledged. Pregnancy loss is a life-changing event. Because we are changed, it makes no sense to ignore what changed us.

Many couples who experience pregnancy loss hear "Never mind. Try again, dear," or "It's not as if you *knew* the baby. You'll get over it." Comments such as these do not make us feel better. They make us feel more isolated and lonely because the person who said them has closed the door and said, "I don't want to hear any more about how you feel."

It may be true that we can carry on, but the loss is not diminished by ignoring it. In an article entitled, "Those Babies Were Real," a mother wrote in *Treasury of Celebrations*, "It is strange that an infant, wanted or unwanted, planned or unplanned, an infant not even properly born, let alone named, can affect a person. It has been almost 20 years since my five-day-old daughter died, and almost 25 years since a miscarriage, but those babies changed the way I see love and life, children, the world, and myself.

"I think now it is a mistake not to properly grieve infants or fetuses who die. Somewhere inside (and from society) we hear the message that 'we didn't know them – it's not as if they were real.' And so, we 'buck up'; we 'get on with life.'

"But they were real. They changed my marriage, my faith, my outlook on life, my other children's lives. If I had to do it over again, I would have a funeral or make up a ritual of loss. I would gather together the people who loved me and ask them to weep and wail with me. I would forget about being brave until all my tears had fallen.

"I am sure that no one outside my immediate family remembers those babies. But I do. They changed me."

In our culture, there is little acknowledgment of pregnancy loss, and usually no formal ceremony.

When Janice Bjorkman of Wisconsin learned she was pregnant with their third child, she was guardedly happy and more than a little apprehensive. She was 39 years old. As her pregnancy entered the sixteenth week, she and her husband drove to the hospital for an ultasound and amniocentesis.

"We were thrilled to see images of our baby on the screen." But in less than a week, test results confirmed Down's syndrome. A second ultrasound revealed heart and kidney problems. "In an instant our world changed. We at first thought that we surely could handle a Down's child, but with all of the other problems, we wondered about her quality of life. The anguishing decision was made to set her free from an earthly life of pain and uncertainty and to terminate the pregnancy." Janice checked into the hospital on Thursday and the procedure was to have ended on Friday. It took until Saturday.

"When Ellen was born, the nurses took her and cleaned her up and brought her back to us wrapped in a swaddling blanket. We spent as much time as we wanted and needed, holding her in our arms, naming her after her two great-grandmothers, praying for her, saying good-bye. We committed her spirit into Jesus' hands, in essence baptizing her. Then they took her away, giving us a blanket, a little baby hat, a seashell, and a birth certificate with her tiny footprints on it. My husband had already arranged and paid for the cremation.

"Sobbing, gut-wrenching sobbing, was all I knew for the next few weeks. The pain was just so great and never-ending... Not only was I left with an overwhelming sense of guilt, but my body was thrown unnaturally into postpartum depression. There was no baby to give the joy to help lift me from the depression.

"Ellen died in January. In September we had the memorial service for her. We had kept her ashes in our bedroom closet for those nine months and we were finally ready to commit them and her spirit to God.

"I typed up the service, taking bits and pieces from books, pamphlets, the Bible and planning songs with which my children were familiar. My children didn't seem to want to be part of this, so I asked them to find one thing that they wanted to give Ellen during the service. We went out in the boat, just our family of four. We did the service, singing, praying, and tossing the ashes into Lake Michigan. We got through it somehow, and headed back to shore. It was emotionally draining at the time, but looking back on it [3 years later], it did serve as a comforting closure."

Sources for the music used in this service are listed in the Appendix.

Service of Committal for Ellen Linnea Bjorkman

Opening:
There will be storms in your life – this Jesus promises.
There will be pain and sorrow – this is as unavoidable with you as it was with Christ when he was in this world.
There will never, however, be a moment when God ceases to care about you.
Call to Worship: "Kum ba yah" (Come by here, my Lord) traditional
Prayer: (for God's Presence with Us)
Music: "How Deep Is Your Compassion" by Tracy Danz and Bob Stromberg
Scripture: Psalm 40:1-3
Music: "Children of the Heavenly Father" by Lina Sandell
Scripture: Romans 8:36-39
Time of Silent Prayer
Committal
Prayer
Sending of Gifts
Music: "Jesus Loves Me" by Anna Bartlett Warner
Prayer
Poem: You Will Exist by Janice Bjorkman
To us you will exist
in the flowers
in the trees
in the mountains
in the seas
and all things of nature
God has given us.
You are now in a world of peace and happiness forever.
Pray for us as we pray for you,

and somewhere,
sometime we shall join you.
Music: "Thy Holy Wings, Dear Savior" by Lina Sandell
Musical Benediction: "On Eagle's Wings" by Michael Jonas
Closing: This service has ended, but our life in Jesus Christ our Lord goes on. Amen.

It may be that there are no ashes for a committal service. It may be that the mother was too ill at the time to participate in any ceremony, or that, at the time, "bucking up and getting on with it" seemed the right thing to do. But it is never too late to acknowledge grief or loss.

Sample Ritual for Pregnancy Loss

You may decide to hold this ritual in a beautiful place outdoors, in your backyard, in a chapel, or your front room. You may do this with a group of family and friends; and if faith is important to you, you may wish to adapt this ritual within that context and create it with your clergy.

Ahead of time, ask people to bring a small bottle of water. Before people arrive, place a large bowl and a hand towel in the center of your meeting place. You may wish to play music on a cassette recorder.

Gathering and Welcome
Prayer and/or Reading: Psalm 102:3-7
A Statement of Grief:
We gather together as a human family to mourn the loss of one of us. We gather to offer our love and support to (*parents' names*). We gather in sorrow and in hope.

Humans suffer and endure loss. We survive to live with joy because God's presence is revealed by the people who love us, surround us and offer us support. Today we offer our support to our sister (*name*) and brother (*name*) in the loss of their baby. Although there are often logical, rational medical explanations for loss of pregnancy, these only explain the loss to our brains. Our hearts still do not understand. Our hearts still break with sadness. We are gathered to say that we grieve with you and offer you our love. May the love of the Creator sustain you. May the courage of the Christ carry you from this day into the future. May the everlasting energy of the Holy Spirit give you peace. May the Creator bless each one of us.

The Ritual of the Water: *Invite each person to come forward and pour their water into the bowl. As each person does this, he or she makes a statement to the bereaved couple.*

When everyone has done this, invite them to dip their fingers into the water and place their hands on the couple's shoulders or heads for the following prayer:

Blessing
(*name*) and (*name*), we offer you our support and our blessing. May you grieve together, may you heal together, may you love together, may you know joy together. Amen.

Alternative Ritual of the Water: *Invite each person to make a statement to the bereaved couple. When everyone has done this, invite the couple to hold their hands over the bowl. Then ask each person to pour their water over the couple's hands in a ritual of cleansing the pain they are feeling. When everyone has done this, one person reads the Blessing above.*

Closing: a simple statement by the parents and/or the leader, and appreciation for people's attendance.

Death of a Baby

When she was a student chaplain at Scarborough Centenary Hospital in Toronto, Ontario, Reverend Michele Bland conducted her first funeral – for a stillborn baby.

"It was really sad," she recalls. "I conducted the funeral at the hospital chapel. There were the usual things: music, word of God, and message. The baby, whom the parents had earlier named, was present throughout the service. Prior to the funeral and at the end, the parents were given time to be with their baby. It seemed important to them to have time to hold, cuddle and caress their baby. (With this in mind, it is important that the body is at room temperature.)

"The parents took photographs of the baby, and family photographs of them holding the baby," Michele says. "Since there were so few memories for these parents, it was important to give them as many tangible items as possible. They were given a certificate of birth and death which included an ink stamp of the baby's hands and feet, a lock of hair, the blanket and bonnet the baby wore, an identification bracelet and a copy of the order of service.

"I trust that these extras were helpful in their grieving. I believe that pastoral care and follow-up is vital. Although the situation seemed so sad, it seemed really special to give the parents tangible objects for their remembrance."

In their book *Lights of Passage*, authors Wall and Ferguson tell the story of young parents whose six-month-old daughter died in a traffic accident. Months after the funeral, the parents continued to mourn deeply. They decided to create a ritual for themselves that involved candle lighting and planting a tree in their back yard. The tree roots were wrapped in one of their daughter's blankets.

Planting as a ritual, as a sign of hope and as a gift to the universe can be healing. Many people do this on the anniversary of a death.

The Death of a Child

After Jim Taylor's son Stephen died, he wrote a book called *Letters to Stephen: A Father's Journey of Grief and Recovery.* In it he quotes another bereaved father, Reverend William Sloan Coffin of New York, who wrote, "When parents die, as my own mother did recently, they take with them a large portion of the past. But when children die, they take away the future as well. That is what makes the valley of the shadow of death so incredibly dark and unending."

A funeral for a child is different from other funerals for that reason, and because in our culture, it is unusual. A third circumstance that makes this funeral different, is that there will likely be several young people the child's age in attendance. In planning a child's funeral, we need to keep these things in mind, in addition to the grief and loss that all other death ceremonies acknowledge.

Allan Jones of Oyama, British Columbia was a sports enthusiast and volunteer fire fighter with an infectious laugh. He was 21 years old when he died of an aneurysm in 1996. His mother, Lindy, says that Allan's friends were an important part of the funeral service and the preparation for it. "We were conscious that there would be many, many young people in the church – his teammates and former teammates over the years, former classmates, cousins, friends, and my husband's high school students…six of my son's best friends were picked to usher. They wore his hockey team's bright blue shirts. His best friend took the names we suggested and talked to the other boys for us. Other friends coming in the door also grabbed shirts and helped out. At the time, we felt that my son would have been pleased if all his friends had come in roller-skating down the aisle and body checking each other, but we did draw the line before that.

"Special sections of the church were saved for his hockey team and the local volunteer fire department. His friends made a display of some of his personal items, hockey shirts, army keepsakes, a beer mug from

Germany, team pictures and so on, and set it up in a corner of the church hall for people to look at during the coffee time. They weren't necessarily things that I would have picked, but I did mind my own business. His friends wanted and needed something to do.

"Most of the local young people disappeared after they came through the receiving line, grabbed some food, then went to play an honorary game of pick-up roller hockey at the local tennis court. Those not playing, watched. [Allan had been rushed from this tennis court to the hospital.] I noticed that this was one way that the people his age expressed their grief. There were a lot of honorary games in the next couple of weeks. Playing out their grief in action helped them."

Lindy Jones and her husband and daughters realized they needed to give some leeway to her son's friends who were so important in his life. In other words, they shared their very personal grief. When an older child, or an adult child dies, the very intimate connection between parents and child and siblings and child is different than if the child were quite young.

Ursula Lewis' daughter, Cathy, was married, living thousands of miles away and was herself a mother when she died of a brain tumor. Cathy's funeral, of course, was arranged by her husband and friends.

"When our daughter died she had been living in California with her husband and daughter," Ursula says. "They lived in a very close community called The Free Daist Communion Church with a guru as their master. We were with her the last three weeks and were able to nurse her at home with the help of her loving and caring community. Although outsiders are not normally allowed in a *Puja*, they welcomed us. That was a gift. They informed us of their customs so we were prepared for what followed.

"One of the devotees read from a book by their master, which in a nutshell, was to send Cathy's spirit on to the way it should follow, not to look back or regret, but in simple words, 'to go toward the light.' This went on for at least an hour while we all sat around her bed.

"Three of us prepared her for burial, washing her and anointing her with jasmine oil and wrapping her in a wonderful flame-colored shawl sent especially by their master from Fiji. About an hour and a half later Cathy's friends started arriving to share in the *Puja* which followed. Two women from the sanctuary, dressed in white, prepared incense and flowers, gifts for their master. We sat around the coffin, which was decorated with flowers. She looked beautiful. One of the children played a portable harmonium and they sang chants. Verses were recited and we were all touched with some holy ashes and sprinkled with holy water.

"There was an around-the-clock vigil for three days. The room was kept cold and dry ice was placed under Cathy's shroud. As devotees arrived from the county, they meditated in this room with her. We were allowed to come and go as we pleased. We provided flowers which people placed around Cathy or on the little altar in front of a large photo of their master. The purpose of the vigil was to assist her spirit to go on to wherever God wanted it to go. Cremation followed."

Ursula and Dick returned home to Canada. Ursula says that a dear friend could see that there had been nothing for them at the California service and suggested they needed to complete things. They decided to have a memorial service on the anniversary of Cathy's death. "This was a wonderful solution to our grief, and the planning helped our healing," Ursula says. "We took lots of long walks and talked and planned.

"We contacted our minister and he was all for it. Because Cathy was such a free spirit, we asked him to use Spirit as the theme. Our niece in Montreal, who is more like a daughter, came and sang the song she composed for Cathy when she died. She also gave the Recollections [telling stories of their life together]. A friend read Scripture. A journalist who writes tributes to people who have "made a difference" wrote an article about Cathy in the newspaper.

"Because Cathy loved the exotic, we ordered birds of paradise and other tropical flowers. I made a collage of Cathy's pictures so people could see who she was. We also used a tape of Cathy's organ music, *Toccata and Fugue in D Minor* by J.S. Bach.

"The whole service," Ursula says, "was a celebration."

When a grandparent dies we feel their absence at special events in our lives. For bereaved parents and siblings, the funeral marks the end of the life, and the beginning of a lifelong process of learning to live without the physical presence of the child. When a child dies, we feel their absence when they should have been starting school, graduating, playing on the peewee team, getting married, having children...all the future celebrations have been snatched away.

In *Treasury of Celebrations,* a bereaved mother wrote, "Learning to live with the death of a child is best done in the presence of other bereaved parents. In small or large groups, you will likely discover that what the rest of society might call strange or bizarre is very much normal. You will likely hear about personal rituals that help people readjust to life. To the uninitiated, some rituals may appear unusual, but they seem to maintain a necessary connection with the deceased and to offer creative and personal expressions of a grief that has no equal. These rituals are expressed most often on the anniversary of the child's death, on the child's birthday, on the first day of school, and during 'regular' celebrations such as Christmas, Hanukkah, Halloween, Easter, Mother's Day, and Father's Day.

"Rituals include writing periodic letters to the child, visiting the grave site, giving a gift to a library or school on the birthday in memory of the child, hanging the child's Christmas stocking and having members of the family write notes to the child to place in it, burning special candles during the holidays or on some special date, decorating a small Christmas tree and placing it on the grave site, making a quilt in memory of or with the clothing from the deceased, and so on.

"Many bereaved parents agree that the most difficult time of the year is December; perhaps this is why rituals are more important then. In December, nondenominational candlelight services are held annually by chapters of The Compassionate Friends, an international organization of bereaved parents and siblings. At this service, the children are remembered with candles and flowers, and their photographs are displayed."

When a child dies, people learn to live with it, rather than "getting over it." Parents learn to say good-bye over and over again, sometimes alone, sometimes with others, repeatedly re-creating themselves as they go along.

Sample Memorial Ceremony for a Child

Place one large white candle on a table in the center of your circle. Near it, place photographs and/or mementos of your child.

Words of Welcome
Reading: Lament
for Michael and Kathryn

Are you there, God?
It's me.
I need to hear your voice
Need to feel you wipe my tears
Gently.
Are you there, God?
I need to learn to redefine my life.
I need to redefine
Worth
Beauty
Time
Friendship
Love
Family...
Are you there, God?
Help me, loving mother, loving father,

Help me redefine what it means to be
Whole.
Add your breath to mine
as I cry out for hope in this
strange, new, old place.
 – *Carolyn Pogue. This poem first appeared in* The Calgary Herald.

Reading: Psalm 139:1-18
Light the candle.

Statement about the Purpose of the Gathering: Today we gather
to remember *(name)* as a group of people who miss him/her and as
people who love this family, so deeply hurt by loss. We had heard about
the Valley of the Shadow of Death. Now we see what the walls of the
valley look like. We know the treacherous path because our feet stumble
on it. We feel how dark and cold and deep this valley is. May we also
understand the shadow in this valley. May we remember what causes a
shadow.

We are not alone in this valley. We are here together. May we reach
out a hand.

May we also remember that the cause of deep grief is deep love.
And it is our deep love for *(name)* that brings us together today.
Music: Lullaby (for a deep sleep)
for Catherine Lewis 1947-1994

You lie here in my arms, Your head upon my thigh.
I look upon your face, I stroke your brow.
Your lips begin to move, the words float out in song
Like ribbons in the wind they float away.
These words your song
A life that must be told,
A life that must let go.

A stranger who is with you on the fires of souls
A stranger who is witness to these silver hours.
A stranger who will listen to your final words.
Let them go.
If you have lies, if you have secrets
If you have promises unkept,
Let them go.

If you were unloved, if you were abandoned
If you were all the gifts this world can give
Let them go.
Let it float upon the currents into shore
Let your body give itself to evermore
Let the perfume of this world
Take your limbs and make them weightless
Let them go.

You lie here in my arms your head upon my thigh
I watch you as you float away from shore.
I let you go.

by Barbara Lewis copyright 1994
(See Appendix A to order music tape and CD.)

Invitation for the gathered to offer memories of the child
Invitation for the gathered to offer words of affirmation and comfort to the bereaved family

Music Selection
Reading: In Nazareth
Mary, your fingerprints
    Must be here somewhere,

Your breath
    Must hang in the troubled air;
Your footprints
    Must linger on cobblestones,
Where I now
    touch
            breathe
                    stand.

I am looking for a miracle
    Solace
I am searching for
    Comfort
In the bewildering, raging storm
That you and I share
Grieving for our
Sons.
    – *from* Unholy Poems *by Carolyn Pogue*

Prayer for Comfort
Gentle God,
    We bring you our pain and lay it in your lap. It is too big for us alone. We bring you our memories, our broken hopes, our rage. Take these things into yourself. Transform them for us in the greatness of your heart, so that we can re-create ourselves with new ingredients made from them.
    We remember Mary of Nazareth, whose own son died before her eyes. We remember parents in the Holocaust. We remember Central American Mothers of the Disappeared. We call on the spirit and the courage of these women and men to be with us, to guide us, to sustain us in the time to come. Amen.

Music Selection
Benediction:
Our illusions have been stripped away;
    may we not replace them with bitterness.
Our lives have been touched by tragedy;
    may we go forward carrying gentleness.
Our world has been altered profoundly;
    may we face the future enabled to love simply.
Our wholeness has been shattered;
    may we learn anew what wholeness can be.
May the love of friends and family sustain us.
May the presence of our compassionate Creator go with us. Amen.

SIX

SUICIDE

His words are a blur,
the sheer weight of the message crushes their fragile memory.
I know he broke it to me in stages...
I only remember asking two questions.
One was whether or not he was dead
and the other was whether he'd done it by shooting himself
in the head."
Sue Chance in *Stronger than Death*

"There are no specific rituals or customs for death by suicide," a survivor told me. "The usual murmurings don't necessarily help; the reaction of family and friends cannot be relied upon." Even though the families and friends of 3,709 Canadians and 30,484 Americans were confronted – in one year – with the death by suicide of someone they loved, as a society we are left practically speechless by it.

Survivors of suicide face the reality of death differently than do the survivors of other deaths. They not only face the loss of a family member, but must also deal with the shock of sudden death and the trauma and/or stigma associated with suicide.

In his book, *After Suicide,* John H. Hewett raises an important point about how we name this death. "Committed" is a word that usually introduces a sin or a crime. By saying "committed suicide" we are judging the act. And yet, people who attempt or complete suicide are people who are in pain. Hewett suggests that we use the term "completed suicide," rather than "committed." People left in the wake of suicide need understanding and comfort every bit as much as any other bereaved child, parent, sibling, spouse or friend. The need for reassurance may be even greater than for other bereavements. Changing our terminology can perhaps, in a small way, begin to offer that reassurance.

After her husband completed suicide, one woman told me, her concern centered on her 11-year-old daughter who was convinced that her daddy was going to hell. "I don't know where she got it," the mother told me. "I immediately called our minister who came over and reassured her. It was important that the reassurance came from 'the church.'" Sixteen years later, the woman commented, "Our society is harshly judgmental."

For years, survivors will ask, "Why?" Society's attitude compounds the question. Debbie Weir, writing in the *Killivaq News* in Rankin Inlet, NWT, said, "In this column we proudly announce births and weddings, special visitors and many other great things. Occasionally we also mention the passing away of friends and family. It is a sad occasion when the passing of someone is not mentioned due to the fact that the person has taken their own life.

"This is so again this week in the Keewatin. It is not necessary to mention the name of the person, as the family and friends are experiencing such sorrow words cannot comfort them. It is necessary to mention, though, that suicide is a problem of such magnitude that it is terrifying...Who can help? The answer is no one...and you. Let's talk about it."

Choosing to die rather than face difficult living is an age-old dilemma. Hewett writes it was also a problem for the early Hebrews, Romans and Greeks. In Hebrew scripture we read of Moses, Elijah, Jonah, the writer of Ecclesiastes, Jeremiah and Job lamenting their lives. We read of others who completed suicide, including Saul, but, according to Hewett, we do not read moral comments in scripture about the manner of their deaths. The only recorded suicide in the New Testament is that of Judas Iscariot, and only Matthew records it as a suicide. "The New Testament [writers and editors] and the early church both regarded Judas as a traitor...because he betrayed Jesus, and only for that reason," writes Hewett.

Suicide became a serious problem for the early church. Like others throughout history, some of these persecuted people opted for death. The reason the early Christian church came down so hard on suicide was that it became commonplace.

Condemnation continued for centuries. A pamphlet published by the Mental Health Association in Pewaukee, Wisconsin states that "early

Roman and English laws established suicide as a crime because it was thought a person ended his life to avoid paying taxes!"

For hundreds of years, surviving families have been shunned and refused permission to bury their loved one in churchyards. The legacy of grief was compounded by bewilderment, helplessness, guilt and societal punishment *of the survivors*. In some ways, our society isn't much more enlightened.

"There's more to be sensitive to in this death," says Bill Phipps. "We need to be more sensitive about where the family is. Sometimes, it isn't clear that the death was suicide. Quite often, even if it's clearly a suicide, the family needs time to acknowledge that.

"If it's clear to the family that suicide has occurred, we need to address feelings of guilt that may be present; we need to tackle that honestly and head-on. If a person dies of cancer, families have total and awful grief, but they aren't left feeling guilty about the cancer. With survivors of suicide there are a whole lot of other burdens and questions, such as 'What could I have done to prevent this?'"

He says that in a funeral or memorial ceremony, "I'd likely acknowledge that this is a tragic and untimely death, and that we don't know what happened, really. The family will be struggling to understand this death for a very long time. My job as minister is not to play amateur psychologist. What I think is required of me is to be present to them in their grief.

"It isn't right for one to assume they know how another person feels. My view is, the less said, the better. You might say "You must be in great shock;" that's one thing you can be fairly sure of, but I wouldn't impose any of my feelings on the family.

"Suicide (and the death of a young person) assault our understanding of life as a circle. In these cases, death cuts the circle, and cuts to the heart of our understanding of the natural process of living and of life and death."

One Family's Story

Barb McConnell is of Ukrainian descent. In her family, there are specific death rituals: a prayer service the night before the funeral, a Forty Day Dinner, and a dinner and memorial service on the first anniversary of the death. Having more than one "event" allows mourners to gather in a more or less formal and prescribed way and to "check in" with each other to see how they are coping and adjusting.

Allison McConnell completed suicide in January, 1996. She was 16 years old.

Devastated by this tragedy, her family confronted the manner of her death, and managed to construct a beautiful ceremony in Allison's memory. Allison's brother Chris, 19, worked with his parents in all the arrangements, and co-officiated with the pastor at both services.

Before the evening prayer service, Allison's friends spent time with her body at the funeral home, and left love offerings of jewelry, photos, letters, notes, cards and flowers in the casket. Her mother also placed Allison's teddy bear in the casket. Then the casket was escorted by Chris and the pastor into the main room where the mourners had gathered.

The McConnells brought photo albums and large pictures of Allison and displayed them throughout the funeral and prayer service. Allison's girlfriend offered to bring her string quartet to play in her honor. Another of her friends sang.

During the prayer service, Chris read his own tribute to his sister. The tribute included a slide show of Allison's life. He had also prepared a music tape of Allison's favorite music, and this played during the slide show. "It was a real mix of music," Barb says, "and included country and western music that Allison loved. It was music her friends would enjoy, while taking into account the older people present. The slide show was important," she adds. "We had all seen Allison in death. The slides showed her in life, so the last images people had of her were happy."

Allison's parents had found her diary. Together they composed a final entry and read it during the ceremony:

Dear Journal,

Hi. Well, it's been a while since you have been written to, and this time it is from us, Terry and Barb, Allison's parents, and Chris, big brother and mentor. We are sure you have heard many conflicting descriptions of us, some are true, some were true, but the underlying and most important description is that of three very lonely and confused individuals who have lost someone so dear to them that they cannot even begin to explain. We loved her more than life itself, but could not get it through to Allison, particularly, it would seem, when she needed it most.

Allison's father continued:

"On January 29th, 1996, we lost something that could not possibly be replaced. It's a horrendous feeling of loss, guilt, remorse, sadness and anger. Over the past few days Barb and I have sat in our home trying to reflect and reason why and how such a tragedy could happen..."

In his talk he spoke of his love for his daughter and of her difficulties. He told what it was like to arrive at the hospital and find that Allison had died. And he spoke directly to Allison's friends and their parents:

"Parents, please find your daughter or son, put your arms around them, hold on to them, protect them, cherish them, and most of all tell them how much you love them.

"Children and young adults, when you get home, be with your parents, hug them and tell them how you love them. They may not be as understanding as you would like, but please rest assured they do love you and couldn't bear to be without you. Do this for us and Allison."

Teachers, friends, other parents and other relatives also spoke about Allison. "There was humor, too," Barb recalls.

Because Allison had died by hanging, Allison's family had the presence of mind to request that no one at the funeral wear a tie or anything around their necks. "Even the funeral directors respected this," Barb says.

The funeral, held the following day, repeated some of the readings, music and slide show, and included prayers and a message from their pastor. After the service, the McConnells gave roses to special friends.

The services didn't end with the funeral. According to Ukrainian tradition, the McConnells also hosted a Forty Day Dinner. Forty days after the death, special family and friends gathered to remember. Here, they played the music tape created by Chris, told stories, looked at pictures, talked about how they were managing, and about suicide and teenage depression.

A week after that, the McConnells invited all Allison's friends to their home. They knew they were still mourning, too, and that they had unanswered questions. The teenagers were welcomed and were free to wander the house, sit in Allison's room, look at pictures and ask whatever they wanted. "If I couldn't answer the question," Barb says, "if it was too difficult just then, I told them that I would have to answer it later. And that was okay."

The McConnells also asked a priest to bless Allison's grave. This also is a Ukrainian tradition, conducted annually. People might lay a basket containing bread and fruit, or mementos (Barb took some guardian angels) on the grave, so they are blessed as well. "Afterward, I gave those things to people I love, in Allison's memory," Barb says.

"On her birthday, I made some cross-stitch pictures and gave them, along with Allison's picture, to friends. I'm still celebrating her life and her memory. The tradition is there, but we change it to suit us, and to suit Allison. The way Allison died has meaning. We have to stop these suicides. The problem I have with suicide is everybody else's feeling about it – the stigma."

Another Family's Story

Fourteen-year-old Ben McMordie ended his life in 1982. The advice his parents received from a neighbor was simple and helpful. "She was an angel of mercy," Ben's mother, Claire recalls. "She said you must think only of yourself. Stop trying to take care of other people and tell me what you need. What I needed was to be alone. I'll never forget her. She had one foot on the front door, another foot on the back door and one hand on the phone and she was saying, 'I'm sorry, no, she can't see anyone right now.' I later found that some people had been excluded, and if I'd been thinking it wouldn't have happened that way, but I wasn't able to think."

The McMordies had a small family service at a funeral home prior to cremation. Two days later, they had an evening memorial service at their neighborhood church. They were overwhelmed by the number of people who came to be with them.

"Both services were brief," Claire says. "I don't think I could have sat up very long at that point. I wrote a eulogy and the minister read it. We sang *Praise my Soul the King of Heaven*. The lines I remember are 'Frail as summer's flower we flourish; blows the wind and it is gone...'"

After the church service, friends and family were invited to her neighbor's home for refreshments. Claire asked the chaplain back to her own home. "I let all families with neighborhood kids who had known Ben know that the chaplain would be there. The neighborhood kids went in and sat on the floor and talked about what they were doing when they found out about Ben's death. The chaplain showed them the room where Ben died and all kinds of things which for some reason I thought were very important for the recovery of our neighborhood – not to have questions festering or a sense of mystification. Someone wrote me a note afterward and said that they could not imagine how I could think of others at a time like this. But it seemed natural."

When the one-year anniversary date approached, the family

retrieved the ashes from the funeral home to dispose of them. Claire and her husband Mike chose a place in the mountains which the family had visited on a camping holiday. A few days before the anniversary, the children, then aged 13 and 8 and their parents hiked to the snow-covered mountain meadow. Each had brought something they wanted to read aloud. They also read from the burial service in The Anglican Church's *Common Book of Prayer,* then spread the ashes in the wind. "When we drove home there was an extraordinary mood of almost quiet celebration – release – a tremendous anxiety was lifted off me after that," Claire recalls. "The children asked us questions then about God and the life after death: Are there basketball games in heaven?"

On the actual one-year anniversary date, friends of the family and of Ben gathered at their home. "We each had a small thing to say. We talked about our struggle as a family. I read a poem that Ben Johnson wrote when his son died. Our son David, who was 8, had written "I like Ben because he babysits and teaches me about science." Claire says that the first-year rituals of placing the ashes and of seeing a few close friends for a structured service seemed to bring "a window of release in the anguish and torment of the first year."

For around 10 years after Ben's death, the family set aside the anniversary date to be together. They canceled work and school, talked about Ben and looked at his photographs. First the children decided that they did not need this ritual any longer, and eventually Claire says she "didn't feel the need to stay home and shelter...the date has lost its power to a great extent."

In recalling that time, Claire says that "there were four angels present to me in the form of friends. My neighbor was one. They all helped differently but most profoundly. Each in a different way gave me strength and endurance because they knew that the suffering would deepen over the foreseeable future, and were able to support me in that."

A year after Allison McConnell's death, her mother says she's learned some things. "People don't know what to say. Nobody teaches death education. In the case of suicide, the survivors are left with the job of educating people. I've also learned that it's not the way my daughter died, or even the reasons for suicide that are important. What's important is, I miss her."

Suicide is like a brutal kick in the head and the stomach simultaneously. Survivors have to concentrate to do the simplest tasks. Because of this, many people have a hard time even remembering the funeral or memorial ceremony. And as Elisabeth Knübler-Ross says, this grief lasts much longer than if the person had died of natural causes. For these reasons, and because support is so important to the bereaved, it seems particularly fitting to consider holding a "One Year Survival Ceremony."

Sample One-Year Survival Ceremony

You may wish to do this in a meadow, on the back lawn, in your living room or a chapel.

Invite everyone to bring a short reading from material already written or an original piece about courage. Choose appropriate music that is reminiscent of the one who has died and/or music that is soothing. In the center of your circle, place three unlit white candles, a photograph and memento of the deceased, and something that for you, symbolizes courage. (This may be a plant that flourishes in adverse conditions.)

Welcome the guests
Statement of Purpose for the Gathering
One year has gone since *(name)* passed from our lives. In these very long and very short 12 months, we have traveled a distance greater than we could have imagined. We have changed. We have grown. We have walked through the Valley of the Shadow of Death that the shepherd-king David spoke of thousands of years ago. We have lost, but we have gained, too.

Today we are together to remember *(name)* and to say to one another: "You are strong. You have walked a hard, long road, but you have arrived here with me. I am grateful."

Light the candles.

Opening Prayer:

Giver of Hope and of Courage,

We come to you knowing we are fragile, and knowing we are strong. We give thanks that we are together now, here in this place. We give thanks for your presence among us always, and especially in the past difficult months. We ask you to stay close to us now as we remember, as we celebrate the courage that has brought us to this day, and as we feel again the pain of losing our beloved *(name)*. Let us feel your warm embrace. We ask this in the name of all who show courage and grace in the face of disaster, and in the name of your Child. Amen.

Music Selection

Invitation for individuals to read their words about courage

Music Selection

Reading: Resurrection

Standing at the railing on the Vancouver ferry
I can't find the horizon,
Can't distinguish between Earth and sky.
Is this how the angels see life and death –
One misty blue canvas?
I am suspended there:
Hanging between.
Powerless.
Caught.
Which way will I fall?
Inside the cabin
Thirty little kids practice the choral number
They will sing on the mainland.
Old women stare out the windows with wet eyes.

Old men rattle newspapers
Or sleep.
A young couple offers Arrowroot cookies and eyes their toddler
Lest he fall.
They fuss.
If he falls, will he rise again?
I drink ferry-bad coffee and watch again the horizonless blue sky.

Once, I drank life daily; simply lived.
But not anymore. No.
The Valley is deeper than imagination.
So deep I cannot tell which way to go to find the sky.
So deep I am under water,
Under mountains,
Under Earth,
Ah. Sheol.
Here life is more complicated. Thicker.
I have to concentrate in order to keep breathing.

I want to live.
I will myself to breathe freely.
I want to live and love life deeply and fully.
It is fierce, this sudden commitment.
It feels raw, filled with energy.

This is resurrection:
To live when your love has died.
This is resurrection:
Not to quit.
This is resurrection:
What mothers and fathers
Sisters and brothers

Daughters and sons
Lovers and partners
– Survivors –
Do every day.

Resurrection is what
We all do
When we must learn to stitch our futures
With broken thread.

This is resurrection:
To remember birthing my love,
To learn to birth myself,
And sometime,
Midwife the resurrection of another.

I step off the ferry and feel strong.
I touch the Earth knowing
I will have to take this journey again tomorrow
And the next day –
Forever.
The horizon is still blurred –
Only my feet are clear.
For this blessed day,
Just concentrate on them, I think.

   by Carolyn Pogue. This poem appeared in an adapted form in Quest,
vol. 1. No.1, 1995

Reading: Psalm 23
Music Selection
Reading: Someone Who Cares
Take my hand
Let me guide you
I've been here before.
Don't let the darkness and sadness
In your heart swallow you,
Just hold on tight.
You can climb out of the despair
Just hold on! Hold on!
   – by Allison Dawn McConnell, Edmonton, Alberta 1979 – 1996

Closing Words of Appreciation for Support

SEVEN

YOUR OWN
DEATH

Do not refrain from speaking at the proper moment,
and do not hide your wisdom.
Sirach 4:23

For families preparing the funeral of a loved one – you – your written wishes can be a gift that alleviates some of the planning and details. More than that, though, it demonstrates that you know you can't live forever, and that you have some level of acceptance of the inevitable. People who have been through this say that it helped them accept the death better, too. Before getting too carried away about every minute detail, though, it is likely good to remember that in the final analysis, the ceremony is for the living.

This chapter highlights four areas that can help you and your family prepare for your death: ethical wills (or "words to the future"), personal directives (also called living wills), the funeral or memorial ceremony, and disposal of your body. But before getting into that, I'd like to tell you about two wonderful ideas I heard about. One is having a party, and the other is suggesting a memorial hike.

My friend Anne Klaiber told me about a woman who learned she was dying. She threw a party for all her family and friends. She reasoned that they would all likely get together after her death, and she wanted to be there to say farewell in the flesh. Hence, the idea for the party. She surprised everyone by calling it a wake.

She sent out invitations, booked a church hall for Saturday after evening Mass, and asked everyone to bring a joke with them, as well as a donation for the food bank. Evidently, story-telling ran rampant, food was festive and music and laughter were there in abundance.

Anne also told me about the memorial hike that Father Pat O'Byrne suggested his friends take after he died. Everyone who knew this well-loved, outspoken priest was invited, via the newspaper, to pack a lunch, put on their hiking boots and head to Forget-me-not Lake in the Rocky Mountains. At the lake, people participated in a memorial worship and prayer. Father Pat, as he was called, was thinking of what would make his friends feel better after he left them. There's not much that's better on Earth than a hike in the Rocky Mountains.

These ideas may not be practical or possible for you, but they demonstrate the loving thought that two people expressed for their friends and family.

Upon your death, your family and friends will suddenly be required to think of all sorts of details, such as arranging the ceremony, possibly hosting people from out of town, notifying people, consoling one another, preparing meals for additional people and trying to adjust to your physical absence. There are many decisions to be made. Planning for your own death can be a gift to your family and friends; your clear guidelines can relieve pressure on them. If there is disagreement among them, your wishes regarding disposal of your body and the general outline of how you would like your funeral or memorial service to run, can settle some of these matters. It can be satisfying for them to know they're fulfilling your wishes, too.

Some people do write out what they would like at their funeral, or their thoughts regarding life support and living wills, but then pack away the documents and neglect to tell anyone about them. Obviously, it's not helpful to the family to find your wishes a week after the funeral. So writing out what you would like is no more important than making sure that people receive a copy.

Memorial Society

A memorial society is a nonprofit group that can help you plan your funeral. Their mandate is to offer help in securing an economical ceremony and disposal of the body. Run by boards of directors, there are 175 member groups in Canada and the USA. If you become a member of a memorial society, they will provide information about cremation, burial, body donation, talking about death with your family, funeral arrangements, costs, estate planning, wills, power of attorney, financial help and more. You can take your time making decisions and plans, then file them with the society, and keep one copy for your family. If you change your mind about certain things or move, you notify them. (See Appendix A for their main address.)

Ethical Wills (or Words to the Future)

Last year I was in a group looking at Paul's epistles in the Bible. These are letters that the apostle wrote to his friends in the brand new churches emerging about 2,000 years ago. When you think of them in the light of letters to friends, they seem much more approachable. He was dealing with issues about which the churches were in conflict. He was trying to tell them what he believed about life and death. He was casting out ideas about how to live. Imagine someone reading your mail years after you are dead! As an exercise, everyone in our group was given the task of writing 25 words to the future generations. What was important to us? What did we believe about life, about death, about God? It was fun!

Some of us write our wills to distribute our bank accounts, our rocking chairs, our paintings, our jewelry. But not many of us think about what is written in our hearts, and passing that on in written form.

In her book, *Put Your Heart on Paper: Staying Connected in a Loose-ends World,* author Henriette Anne Klauser writes about Rabbi Vicki Hollander. Rabbi Hollander is a bereavement coordinator in a hospice. She calls on her Jewish tradition of encouraging people to write ethical wills. The book describes in detail how others have written ethical wills. Some are general; others are to a specific child, for example. Some may take the form of memoirs, others may be letters. To help get you started, you might consider the following:

I believe that _____

I am grateful for _____

I regret that _____

I live in hope that _____

I hope to be remembered for _____

In the past few years, I have learned that _____

What I wish most for you is that _____

If I had my life to live over, I would _____

Living Wills or Personal Directives

Our grandparents certainly didn't have to deal with this one! In the "old days," people lived or died, it seems. Now babies born too soon and people trapped in comas can receive technological care. Medical "miracles" abound. But somewhere in between miracle and mayhem, we are sometimes forced to make difficult decisions. Living wills deal with the question of whether to prolong life through medical intervention or whether to allow nature to take its course.

In addition to the marvels of medical science making prolonged life (or prolonged death) possible, a second matter has changed in this generation. For the most part, our doctors do not know us personally. Today when we become seriously ill or injured, the chances are good that we'll be treated by a stranger who does not know us, or our values. Furthermore, in the booklet *Preserving Dignity – Personal Directives* we read, "When in hospital, physician and nurse will change several times...because of patient transfer to another service, or because one goes off service and another comes on. This fragmentation of acute hospital care is now the norm."

Few of us know ahead of time if decisions will need to be made for us. We don't have many guidelines. Ethics and spiritual direction lag behind scientific technology and its ability to thwart death or prolong the dying process. Although there are scenarios all over North America every day in hospital rooms where families and physicians quietly make life and death decisions, legally the effect of such decisions may be uncertain (depending on where you live). As a society we remain unsure of where we stand.

It is important to discuss your wishes with your family, your doctor, lawyer, and clergy person or spiritual director. Booklets guiding you through the process of filling out a form may be available from your clergy or from a hospital. My parents have given this question consideration. On a recent visit they showed me handwritten notes (which they carry in their wallets), asking that "all reasonable avenues for prolonging qualitative life be tried," but that common sense must prevail. More important, they have discussed the issue with their children and said they do not want "heroics" at the end of their lives.

Jack and Ruth Newell were on a world cruise when he became ill. He had been working on a family history book, *To Kid, A Love Story*, as a gift for his family. He did not live to see his book completed and published. Jack was diagnosed with a fast-acting type of cancer. Ruth Newell writes, "We still didn't know what decision Jack would make [about chemotherapy]. It was only because he thought that he might get two months that he decided to go for it. He hoped that he would be able to finish his manuscript.

"Within a few days he really started coughing. Medication kept being added and changed daily. The nightmare was in progress...

"...He was attached to oxygen and an IV with antibiotics. Because of the massive dose of chemo Jack had been given, his white cells were almost knocked out, leaving him with 300 instead of 3,000. His poor immune system couldn't handle it. Pneumonia set in.

"Jack had nothing to eat for the ten and a half days he was a patient. He was losing weight at a great rate. Oxygen was increased until he was administered 70 percent...

"Jack and I had made out 'living wills' some time ago. Dr. Groves had a copy. Jack had said to him, 'No heroics, Terry.'

"By Sunday we were all showing fatigue, and a family conference decided that we would share the nights so that we could each get a few hours sleep. I felt that we had to stop Jack's oxygen, because that was what he wanted, however, the time had to be right for him – and for me to live with the decision.

"After taking a couple of hours' rest down the hall, I returned Monday at 3:00 am. [Son] Chris was resting in the room. Jack was very restless. The oxygen mask seemed such a nuisance with water gathering in his nose. Jack didn't like it; he wanted it off. We took it off and Chris just held the hose. As we were about to put it back on, Jack waved his hand to tell us 'it was time.' We left it off."

During the morning, the family gathered again, and Jack's daughter shaved him. Ruth wrote, "He was so at peace... Jack's breathing became ever so shallow. Then we realized he had died. What a peaceful way to die..."

Two years later, Ruth observed that she was relieved they had both made living wills. They had given a copy to each of their adult children and discussed it with them, answering any questions that arose. They also gave copies to their doctors. "I think it makes it easier for the kids if a doctor is involved," she says. "Especially if there's discord in a family, the doctor can help in that area."

It is possible to purchase forms to express your wishes regarding living wills. You can also speak to your lawyer about this, or handwrite your wishes as my parents have done. Depending on where you live, a living will or personal directive may be a valid and binding legal document, or it may simply be a statement of your wishes that you hope will have a persuasive influence on your family and doctor. A lawyer can tell you about the relevant law in your area.

Living Will or Personal Directive (sample)

To: (names of partner, children, other)

_____

My Physician's name, address and phone number

_____

My Lawyer's name, address and phone number

_____

My Executor's name, address and phone number

_____

I make this statement to my loved ones_____
and_____ and to my doctor _____
in an effort to assist them in making decisions about my life and death if
necessary. My hope is that you will allow my life to proceed if some quality is
maintained. However, if the time comes when there is no reasonable
expectation of recovery from illness or accident, then I request that pain be
relieved through medication and that I be allowed to die rather than be kept
alive artificially. I consider being kept alive by machinery when there is great
pain, deterioration, dependence, or hopelessness, not to be life, but rather a
living death.

I am in sound mind today and if I become unsound, let this document express
my feelings about artificial life.

_____

I would consider the following situations to be unacceptable forms of "living":

_____

_____

Additional comments: _____

_____

_____   _____

date   name

_____   _____

witness   signature

_____

witness

Copies to: _____

_____

_____

My Funeral or Memorial Ceremony

Many of us do not consider what our loved ones might like at their ceremony until we are in the throes of planning it and a clergy asks, "Did your mother have any favorite scriptures?" "Did your dad like any particular piece of music?" "Were there any poets your husband especially enjoyed?" "What do you think your wife's happiest accomplishment was?"

It's a strange phenomena, but talking about the end of your life often enriches the present moment. For example, what *are* your favorite readings and music? Is your family aware of these? What do you most want people to remember about you? What passion do you have that has shaped how you view life? What do you believe that spirit is? Planning a funeral – yours, or another's – requires soul searching. And surely that is not a bad thing!

Like living wills, your wishes regarding your funeral or memorial service may not be legal documents, but they are a gift, meant to help your family. Remember that both are useless unless you discuss your wishes with your family.

Your decisions will be influenced by your religious beliefs, or absence of them, and your belief or unbelief in an afterlife. You may want to think about funerals you have attended in the past and ferret out what you liked about them, and what you didn't like. In your opinion, what makes a funeral "good"?

Following is a list for your consideration:

I would like the following written on my tombstone or placed as a memorial in the newspaper _____

I would like no/some/lots of flowers_____

Rather than send flowers, please ask people to donate money to:

_____

The names of people I hope will attend my ceremony are:

_____

I would prefer a formal/informal ceremony _____
Because I am a member of a lodge/fraternity/service/ order/sorority,
namely _____, I would like them to conduct a ceremony
according to our tradition. The person to contact is:

_____.

During the Ceremony

The person I'd like to conduct the ceremony is _____
I would like someone to read the following scriptures, poetry, story

_____
I would like someone to tell the story about_____
I would like someone to sing _____
I would like everyone to sing_____
I would like a choir or group to sing _____
I would like instrumental music to include _____
I would like recorded music to include_____
I'd like you to display the photo of _____, which is located:

_____

Funeral

I would prefer an open/closed casket.
I hope that you will dress me in _____
I hope you will bury me with my_____

Memorial Service

I would prefer no urn present at all _____
I hope you will display my_____(photos, mementos)
    If you would like to write the actual ceremony, see Chapter 4.

Disposal of My Body

There are three usual ways in which a body is disposed of: cremation, burial, and donation for research. This is perhaps one of the most difficult decisions that families make, but there are no easy choices, only choices one can live with. You will help your family by letting them know how you feel now.

Today approximately 80 percent of bodies are buried. The trend is shifting, partly because people are comparing the economics of cremation to burial. People are also expressing more interest in donating their bodies to a research facility as a way of making a contribution to society.

Many people now consider donating parts of their bodies for transplant, before disposal. Because of saving another's life or sight, one's death is perhaps softened. (For more information about donation for transplant, please see Chapter 9.)

Burial

Perhaps one reason people prefer burial is that it slows the process of the emotional parting from the body. One does not face the reality of death of a loved one on Monday and emotionally part with the body on Thursday. It takes some time.

On another level, burial in a cemetery can provide a place for the family to meet, to remember, to *go* when they need to. Visiting the gravesite can be a helpful way to work through grief. Planting flowers and tending them has helped many people through dark days of loneliness. Because a cemetary is usually quiet and often pretty, it can be a reflective place to heal.

Some favor burial because they believe that "returning to Earth" is a natural process. In *The Rituals Resource Book*, author Susan Mumm cautions against this belief. She writes that many cemeteries require the purchase of a metal, fiberglass or cement vault. The casket is placed in it. The vault prevents the casket from decomposing and thereby allowing the ground above to sink.

Cremation

Cremation is often chosen by people who are concerned with the economics of disposal, and by those who find cemeteries and grave markers depressing. Often, they do not wish any marker, but prefer that their remains be "scattered" in a beautiful natural location, like my mother, who says, "under the rose bushes, honey."

Cremation is also chosen by people concerned about the overcrowding in cemeteries.

Donation for Research

As mentioned above, some people wish to make this choice in order to contribute to society, even in death. This choice usually requires no financial cost, (although there could be a charge if a great distance is involved). If you phone your local university, you are liable to speak to a friendly soul, as I did at the local university. He explained that the university is offered approximately 100 bodies each year, and that they are able to use most of them.

Not all bodies can be accepted, depending on the cause and manner of death. (For example, if an autopsy has been performed, if embalming has been done by a funeral director, or if death was caused by disease or accident of such a nature as to make medical study impossible. You need to have an alternative plan, in other words.)

The Department of Anatomy will send you a pamphlet that outlines procedures and provides forms for you. One form is to be sent in now, and three forms are for the time of death. It is important, the pamphlet states, that if you wish to bequeath your body, you should inform your lawyer and have the information in your will. Your next of kin and executor should all know about your desire.

When you die, your family will contact the university as soon as possible. Time is important. Next, the family will go to the facility to sign the required legal documents. After that, the university will go to the hospital to claim the body. The family need have nothing more to do. But they can.

I was glad to hear that the final disposal is performed in a respectful and grateful way in an ecumenical service of committal about every four years. If your family wishes to have the ashes returned to them, they need to tell the university at the time of death.

Otherwise, the bodies are cremated separately, and taken in separate containers to a major city cemetery. Hospital chaplains and people concerned with medical research attend a short service of committal and appreciation there. The ashes are then buried.

My Wishes Regarding Disposal

I would like to be buried in _____ located in _____

My next choice would be _____

I prefer to be cremated _____

I would like you to dispose of my ashes by _____

I prefer that my body be donated for research to _____

and I have contacted the research institution about this. I keep that information in _____

If I die out of the country, I prefer that my body _____

_____

EIGHT

LEGAL AND FINANCIAL MATTERS

*Most of us sign a will hoping that our estate plan
will not be carried out too soon.*
Jean Blacklock, lawyer

There are too many families who have quarreled after their parents' deaths. There are too many instances of resentment between siblings that perhaps could have been avoided if the parents had discussed their desire for distribution of material goods and money, had appointed an executor or signed a power of attorney. Maybe conflict is unavoidable if "Mom really *did* like you best." But in the interests of doing your best planning, there are some organizational gifts you can give to people you love.

Sometimes when we decide to "put our house in order," we are ambushed by our families when we try to tell them where the will is, and to whom we want to give our great-aunt's tea service or our original Robert Bateman painting. If your family does this to you, you may want to ask a third party to help you, a friend, clergy, someone who faced the same brick wall when it came to "death talk."

"Stuff"

Not all of us have fat bank accounts to worry about, but it's a sure bet that most of us have some stuff that we really like. Maybe books, music recordings, maybe a favorite chair, the hockey card collection from the 1950s or the cookbook that was passed down from your grandma.

Lois Harding is a retired psychologist and senior citizen. "You don't want to think death is going to hit you. I'm not ready to die yet, but I'm aware of the fact that it's inevitable and that it's getting closer. It makes me determined to do all the things I want before it hits me. And I've got stuff all over the house that I need to look at, and I know I need to do it before too long. I need to think about things I want family members to have. I have a nephew who's very fond of reading. Every Christmas now, he gets some of the books off my shelf. Mostly what I'm trying to do is organize my mind and dispose of things in the right places, so that after I'm gone they're not just going any old place. If there are things I want someone to have, I've got to start thinking about it now."

Wills

In the book, *When You Want Your Wishes Known: Wills and Other Final Arrangements*, Ron DelBene writes, "When couples come to me for premarriage counseling, I ask if they have wills. Young couples usually laugh…" But there is wisdom in his advice. A couple in their 20s may not believe they have a fortune to leave anyone, but they likely do own some things. Further, it will help them discuss an enormously important area in their new life together: finances, and ultimately, life and death.

A will becomes your voice after you have died. Paying attention to what you would like to say, and to whom, can settle your own mind and allow your descendants, relatives and friends to hear your concern for them when they need to hear it most.

Every state, province and territory has its own set of complex laws on wills and estates. A competent lawyer can provide anything from a review of your homemade will to a full-blown estate plan. As in all matters, the cost is not always indicative of good advice. Shop around, talk to friends about how they documented their estate plan, and don't be afraid to ask for a price quote up front. You also have the option of using prepared forms, available under titles such as *Have You Made Your Will? Will and Estate Planning Kit for Canadians*. These are sold in stationery stores.

Each year, check over your will and update it if necessary.

Some wills are relatively straightforward. For example, if a couple was married for 50 years, they might leave everything to one another, then when the second person died, the remaining assets would be divided among the children.

Some wills are complicated. For example, when a gay or lesbian couple is separated by death and the bereaved birth family does not recognize the partnership. Or when two divorced people marry and each brings children into the marriage, then have more children together. Or, consider this story which was told to me by a financial advisor:

"A man married at age 25 and had two children. A few years later the marriage ended. He raised the children, saved a lot of money, secured a good pension, and paid off his mortgage. Then he fell in love again. He remarried about age 47. This man had the feeling that everything he had accumulated until that marriage was for his children. In his mind, the second marriage began a new phase of his life. He didn't believe his new wife should be entitled to any of his accumulated assets; they were to be kept separate and passed on to his children.

"He believed that he and his wife were starting a new joint venture. Whatever money they made as a couple would go to the wife, should he die. Needless to say, the wife wasn't too enamored with that. She didn't get along with the kids, either.

"So, she's not getting any money, she doesn't get along with the kids, and suddenly, her husband is downsized out of a job.

"There seems to be a rule," this storyteller told me, "that these financial plans are never discussed before the marriage. It's always after the honeymoon that people learn about these ideas from their spouse. To complicate matters further, two years into his second marriage, this man discovered he had a potentially fatal illness. His wife, 45, has foregone her career to move around the country with him for two years. He went out to try to buy life insurance so he could leave her some money. The insurance company said they would insure him – for $500 per month *if* he is healthy for three years."

Alberta lawyer Jean Blacklock wrote a word of caution about wills in her newspaper column in *The Calgary Herald* in 1996. Jean focused on people including unusual dispositions in their wills, and cited a case from 1927 (during Prohibition, remember) where a man who had no descendants, died. This man left each Protestant minister and each Orange Lodge in Toronto one share in the O'Keefe Brewery Company! His will was rather eccentric and funny. Apparently he was, too.

Jean says that in some places there are restrictions, such as The Family Relief Act, that may affect the distribution of an estate. This act may have other names in other jurisdictions, but its purpose is to ensure that a will provides "proper maintenance and support" for the person's dependents. A dependent is defined as the spouse, children under 18 and adult children who because of a mental or physical disability cannot earn a living.

There may also be laws about sharing marital property with a separated or common-law spouse. Jean says that "if you have an uneasy feeling that something you would like to do in your will may not be popular," you might consider legal advice.

She further cautions that the "laws about an estate's distribution and administration are generally unique to each province." When people die owning property in more than one province, territory, state or country, the time and expense of administering the estate can be reduced if the person had a will. In some cases, she adds, "it is even advisable to consider a will for each jurisdiction where property is owned."

Probate

Probate is a court procedure to prove the validity of the will. The executor oversees this process. Probate isn't always necessary and isn't always lengthy. It depends on how complicated the will is, the terms of the will or the way in which affairs were left at the time of death. The cost of probating a will varies according to the geographic location and the size of the estate.

Jean adds, "We estate lawyers see a lot of elderly people being persuaded by their 'loving' children to put their assets into joint names to avoid probate. In my view, people need to proceed with caution for a couple of reasons. On death, the joint owner child could say that the assets are all his or hers, leaving the other siblings with nothing, even though this was not intended. Worse, a co-owner child may take advantage of the parent. Both happen regularly. Be careful when putting assets into joint names with non-spouses."

Intestate Death

If you die intestate, that is, without a will, the court will have to appoint an administrator to decide what to do with your assets. Basically, the particular laws of your state, province or territory then determine who gets your assets and in what proportions. Relatives, from close ones to more remote, usually have first priority. In the unusual case that no relatives are found, some part of the government will often get the assets. For example, in Alberta, the estate would ultimately go the province's universities.

Executor

You will want to assign one or more executors to carry out your wishes. An executor is the person responsible for settling an estate after death. You want someone you like and trust, and preferably who is younger than you are. You want the person to be able to work with your beneficiaries, one who is fair, neutral, honest, organized and is not a procrastinator. Your executor will have copies of your will and your living will or personal directive. You will want to make sure your executor understands your values. (Many people name their spouse.)

Some people, if they are expecting family arguments, assign a corporate trustee.

Power of Attorney

A Power of Attorney is a document signed voluntarily by a competent adult authorizing another person or persons to act on her or his behalf in financial and property matters. (This has nothing to do with health or any other care. That is a personal directive.)

A Durable (or Enduring) Power of Attorney simply means that the agreement between those people continues even if the person becomes mentally incapacitated. In some cases, the document is worded so that it *only* becomes effective if and when mental incapacity occurs.

The person to whom you sign over this authority will be someone you trust absolutely, and you will want to talk with a lawyer about the matter. This person will have responsibility for, and control over your property and financial affairs.

Of course, you want to feel free to discuss this matter with the person of your choice, and to ask them if they are willing to act for you. Again, you will want to ask a person younger than yourself. And you will want to think about an alternate, should your first person not be able to perform.

If you don't have a durable or enduring power of attorney in place, if and when you become mentally incompetent, your family or friends may have no choice but to apply to the courts to be appointed as your trustee. This could result in a family argument or involve significant time and expense.

It is important to fill out forms and discuss matters with your doctor, lawyer, clergy and accountant. But it is no less important to discuss them with the people you love.

At the Advisor's Office

Bill Hodgins is a tax and investment advisor in Calgary, Alberta. Many of his clients are now in their 50s and 60s. "Estate planning has come more to the fore," he says, "particularly in the last few years. As baby boomers age, they are seeing people around them dying...and there's nothing like death to get people thinking." Bill says that as his clients age, he sees his business changing. "We're doing more tax planning with estate planning in mind, rather than trying to best the tax man every year."

Sometimes clients learn that they are terminally ill and come to him for advice. "If their affairs have not been organized I generally offer some simple rules:

1. Be sure your spouse is named as the beneficiary on your RSP documents. Your will should confirm this.
2. Your will should provide that all non-RSP investments will pass to your spouse.
3. You may register your home in the name of your spouse. Your will should reconfirm this."

But the way people listen to advice, he says, depends on what stage of grief they are in. They may be optimistic or in denial or in a rage that they have become ill.

"When people learn that they are dying, they really get focused about what's important to them. My advice for people at all stages of life is to get focused now! Get organized. Don't wait until you're 80, or in poor health. You should have life insurance by the time you are 30. You should talk about finances with your family now!"

Bill's final word is from a man who has heard it all, and too often: "When parents die, all the old family rivalries seem to resurface. It's as if one says, 'When you were four years old, you got a bigger bike than I did. Here we are, 40 years later, and you're still looking for the bigger bike!'"

Conclusion

It is unlikely that your survivors can find your documents easily unless you tell them where they are kept. Let them know where you keep your:

- birth certificate
- Social Insurance Number/Social Security Number
- marriage certificate
- safety deposit box keys
- securities and records
- burial plans
- armed service record
- Old Age Security number
- any company pension information
- income tax information
- service club or fraternity information and contact phone number
- will
- living will
- power of attorney
- insurance policies
- mortgages and deeds
- leases
- debts
- bank accounts
- memorial society papers, if you are a member
- instructions about body bequeathal, if applicable
- instructions about organ donations, if applicable
- other important papers
- and the addresses, phone numbers and names of your lawyer, accountant, clergy, if applicable and doctor.

NINE

TRANSPLANTS AND ORGAN DONATION

I was in the waiting room at the hospital.
Allison was dead.
Suddenly, I thought about transplants,
and a great feeling of calm came over me.
Barb McConnell

It's hard to be unaware of the reality of transplants and organ donation today. Dr. Christian Barnard's first heart transplant in the 1960s made headlines around the world. Today, drivers' licenses routinely have a donor form printed on them, and many hospital forms now ask about organ and tissue donation. Many of us know or have heard of someone who has received an organ or tissue transplant. Indeed, the editor of this book is alive today because he received a double lung transplant in 1990.

Major organ transplants – hearts, lungs, kidneys, livers – get most of the publicity. But there are other transplants, too. Sue Holtkamp, PhD., is a counselor and author who has written extensively about the psychosocial aspects of donation. In an article in *Bereavement* magazine, she wrote, "Everyone thinks in terms of organs because these are dramatic transplants. In reality, tissue is terribly important. Heart valves can save lives, and cornea transplants can restore vision. Lives are enhanced every day because someone became a tissue donor. And tissue can be taken from those who die in the traditional way."

Hearing a doctor tell you your loved one is "brain dead" – while you are looking at someone with no apparent illness or damage, or while you are touching the warm hand of someone who appears to be sleeping – is almost incomprehensible. We know that there are children, women and men on waiting lists hoping for new hearts, livers, lungs and so on. But knowing about organ and tissue donations, and actually dealing with the decision at the time and in the years following, are two different things.

Stephen Taylor died in 1983 after a long illness. His parents had previously agreed to donate any usable tissues and organs, and then to release his body to medical science for student training. But when the time actually came, they withdrew the second part of that permission. "He's been through so much," said his mother. "I don't want to put him through anything more."

The sentiment may not be rational, but it is understandable. Death is not a matter of the mind, but a matter of the heart. Donations and transplants are, too. The subject needs discussion within families, and hard information. Many of us will be asked for donations when someone close to us dies. What will we answer? Will we change our mind at the last minute, one way or the other? How do we "do the right thing"? How do we know how we will feel afterward? The emotional stakes are high on both sides of the question.

Stephen Taylor's parents received notification, a month or two after his death, that his corneas had enabled two other young people to see. "It didn't make our grief any less," his father recalled. "But it did give us perhaps the first feeling of thankfulness since he died."

The Morrisons' Story

The Morrison family had a similar experience.

Eleven-year-old Taiya Morrison was active in dancing, gymnastics, soccer and basketball, but her first love was horseback riding. One autumn day, Taiya's horse bolted and Taiya fell off. Although she was wearing a helmet, she sustained severe head injuries.

Taiya's mother, Debbie, recalls that on the way to the hospital she prayed for courage to accept whatever happened.

"In the first hours it looked like Taiya would live, with minimal brain damage," Debbie says. "However, it soon became apparent that it would not be the case. We were approached by a social worker who told us we'd be asked to consider organ donation."

Debbie found herself thinking not only of Taiya, but of her other four children. "At that moment, " she says, "through the depth of my sadness and heartache...I thought about all the other children who were worrying about their sisters and brothers whose deaths could be imminent, and my heart filled with compassion for them. I knew that we had the ability to end the pain and fear that some of them were experiencing. Without discussion, Taiya's dad and I were able to agree to the request.

"After saying our good-byes to Taiya, we went home and that night as the family gathered around, we shared our grief. The only shred of happiness we could feel came from the knowledge that other people were going to be called to life that night. They were going to receive the miraculous call they'd been waiting for. Donating Taiya's organs allowed us the opportunity to experience some joy amongst the pain."

On their first Christmas without Taiya, six new ornaments were added to the Christmas tree. On each one, Debbie wrote what little information she had about each donor recipient.

The Need for Sensitivity –
Information and Discussion

Unfortunately, not all experiences are that satisfactory. Hospital staff can sometimes be insensitive or remiss in providing enough information to families. Families may not know what the procedures are for establishing brain death. It is unlikely families will know in advance what preparations will occur before surgery. They will probably not realize that once they give permission, their time at the bedside will be severely limited and that the bedside activity will increase dramatically, precluding privacy. Time for touch and farewells is limited.

A woman told me that her husband died as a result of head trauma. In the hours between the accident and when his heart stopped, she was approached by a doctor about "harvesting" his organs. "My reaction," she said, "was to want to lunge at his throat and kill him. In retrospect, of course, perhaps organ donation would have been a good idea. I'd only ever vaguely thought about transplants; we'd never really discussed it. There was nothing in my mind at the time except shock, bewilderment and rage."

It is unlikely that many of us have thought through the actual procedures involved. Unless hospital staff provide detailed explanations ahead of time, families may be shocked. Tests performed on the patient to confirm brain death may include ice water in the ears and painful stimuli. Families will be removed from the bedside so that the preparations for surgery can be made. These preparations include attachment to machinery and perhaps the use of eye patches on the patient. The "end time" is interrupted. One woman said, "All of him was our son, not just his brain." Another parent commented, "No one suggested that we return to see him after surgery, no longer breathing, or warm with a beating heart, but an obviously dead body. This might have helped our grieving process somewhat. We were in no condition to think of it ourselves."

Although tissues can be taken from those who die in the traditional way, organs must be alive to have value. This means keeping the heart beating and the blood circulating until the moment of transplant. Hence the name "beating heart donor." Although this is logical, it is not always explained.

Some families have lingering questions, such as why anaesthetics may be used if the patient is brain dead. According to a representative from the Multiple Organ Retrieval and Exchange Program, nerve endings are the last part of the body to cease functioning. (This can take up to 24 hours after the brain has died.) Anesthesia can prevent involuntary muscle reflexes from interfering with the surgery.

Brain death is still a controversial diagnosis. Criteria for establishing it vary between countries. (Japan for example, did not recognize brain death until 1997.) Confirmatory tests may vary, too.

Some families experience guilt and anxiety at the thought that their loved one may have experienced pain or been aware of the operation.

In Canada there are groups for donor families who want to celebrate their "gift of life." However, there is not a group for donor families for whom the donation has been difficult or who would like to make organ procurement easier on families.

Tony and Val Wright of British Columbia have begun an independent study of organ procurement and donor families. The University of Adelaide in Australia is researching these issues as well. The Wrights' work began after the death of their son Jon, and their agreement to donate his organs. Tony and Val believe that more information and support should be available to donor families and that procedures should be made clear. "We believe that because of the desperate shortage of organs, there is a fear that such openness might make things worse. But alleviating fears might eventually increase donations, and it would be the ethical thing to do." From their experience and research, they offer the following advice to donor families:

- Ask questions about what will happen.
- Perhaps wait until the declaration of brain death before giving permission for transplants. (Then you won't worry that care may have been different because of potential organ donor status. Was your loved one treated as an organ donor or as a patient?)
- Tell the hospital that unless their policies and procedures for diagnosis of brain death are made available and explained to you, you will not give permission.

The Wrights' advice to hospitals or organ procurement agencies is:

- Have a leaflet available explaining what happens to a brain dead patient in preparation for, and going into, transplant. This might reduce the number of donations or might not, but it would result in less posttraumatic stress for families who find out the details afterward. Informed decision-making should be the goal.
- Have another leaflet for families, to explain the hospital's criteria for establishing brain death. A family could then follow the process and be reassured that all was done appropriately.

- As in the bereavement organization The Compassionate Friends, have previous transplant donor families available by telephone to give support.

Celebrating Life, Love and Courage

For anyone involved in a traumatic death – whether or not it involves transplant decisions – one of the hardest adjustments is to rediscover gratitude. To give thanks for what was, even though it may never be possible to give thanks for how it ended. On the anniversary of her daughter Taiya's death, Debbie invited family and friends to a "Lovefest." Her invitation read, "You have provided love and support to one or all of us during this past difficult year. Please come and let us honor you, during this celebration of love. We will enjoy music, singing, food and fellowship. You are invited to share poetry, a song, a favorite reading or any item of your own creation that relates to the theme of love."

In 1996, Debbie was one of the speakers at the Kidney Foundation of Canada's annual "Celebration of Courage." This interdenominational prayer service honors organ donors, actual and waiting recipients, professionals and loved ones involved in the transplant process. Their order of service follows.

A Celebration of Courage

Welcome
Hymn: "Gather Us In" by Marty Haugen
Greeting and Opening Prayer
First Reading: Isaiah 43:1-5, 18-19 (read by the mother of a kidney recipient)
Reading: based on Psalm 139
Readings: John 8:12, 9:1-5 and Matthew 5:14-16 (read by a doctor)

Reflections and Storytelling: by a kidney recipient, a double lung transplant recipient, and the mother of an organ donor
Music: "The Lord Bless You and Keep You" by John Rutter
Prayers of Petition: Spoken by a liver transplant recipient, a nurse, a doctor and a waiting kidney transplant recipient
Celebration of Light: Candles were lit by everyone from the Paschal candle while "A New Dawn" was sung by a choir
Word of Gratitude: spoken by hospital transplant coordinator
Closing Prayer
Blessing
Recessional Hymn: "City of God"
(based on Isaiah 9:2-3 and 1 John 1) by Dan Schutte

During a time of shock, few of us are equipped – mentally or emotionally – to make rational decisions about organ and tissue transplants, yet we will live with these decisions for years and years.

One family I have heard of still is not sure they did the right thing in authorizing the hospital's medical staff to terminate the life support systems that kept their 23-year-old daughter alive so that her organs could be donated after she collapsed with a brain aneurysm.

Another family is equally unsure they did the right thing in withdrawing permission for organ donation.

These are not the kind of decisions that should be made on the spur of the moment, and yet we will likely be asked to make up our minds quickly. Time is important, but there is little of it at the moment of decision. Information and honest family discussion are the keys to successful understanding of this important ethical and medical question.

AFTERWORD

In a society that seems preoccupied with a bottom line, we are bombarded daily with warnings, with information, and with facts about our financial health. But there are bottom lines that have nothing to do with money, and that make life fuller, richer, more joyful than any number of dollars can give us: loving relationships, honesty, being alive to the moment. The real bottom line is that life is finite, and that we are free to live it like misers or like the richest people on Earth.

I hope this book has offered some insights into the creative side of ceremonies that help us with the transition called death. That it will encourage you to explore ways to make the rituals and ceremonies your own. That it will inform you about some of the options. I hope that reading other people's stories will offer you alternatives or additions to what may be the norm in your community or experience.

In a world that seems to spin faster and faster, it is my hope that when you face your own death, or the death of someone you love, you will take enough time to slow down, to focus on what is truly important, and to respond in honesty to the language of the heart.

CAROLYN POGUE is a freelance writer and editor. Her work includes plays, articles, poetry, musicals, and short fiction for both children and adults. She has edited several books, including *Treasury of Celebrations: Create Celebrations that Reflect Your Values and Don't Cost the Earth* (1996) for Northstone Publishing. Her most recent book, *Part-Time Parent: Learning to Live Without Custody* was published by Northstone in the fall of 1998.

APPENDIX A
RESOURCES

Bloyd, Sunni. *Euthanasia.* San Diego: Lucent Books Inc. 1995.

Chance, Sue. *Stronger than Death: When Suicide Touches Your Life.* New York: W.W. Norton & Company. 1992.

Cloutier, Kathy. *Customs and Traditions in Times of Death and Bereavement.* Calgary: McInnis and Holloway Funeral Homes. 1996.

DelBene, Ron et al. *Times of Change, Times of Challenge: When You Want Your Wishes Known: Wills and Other Final Arrangements.* Nashville: Upper Room Books. 1993.

Driver, Tom F. *The Magic of Ritual: Our Need for Liberating Rites that Transform Our Lives and Communities.* New York: HarperSanFrancisco. 1991

Fritisch, Julie with Sherokee Ilse. *The Anguish of Loss: For the Love of Justin.* Long Lake, MN: Wintergreen Press. 1988

Fulghum, Robert. *From Beginning to End: The Rituals of Our Lives.* New York: Villard Books. 1995.

Gottselig, Cheryll C. *Wills for Alberta: How to make your own will.* Vancouver: Self-Counsel Press. 1995

Gunderson, Harold. *A History of Funeral Service in Alberta.* Calgary: Alberta Funeral Service Association. 1993.

Haddon, Celia. *Love Remembered: A Book of Comfort in Grief.* London: Michael Joseph Ltd. 1997.

Harpur, Tom. *Life after Death.* Toronto: McClelland and Stewart. 1991

Hewett, John H. *After Suicide.* Philadelphia: Westminster Press. 1980.

Johnson, Christopher Jay and Marsha G. McGee. *How Different Religions View Death and Afterlife.* Philadelphia: The Charles Press Publishers. 1991.

Klauser, Henriette Anne. *Put Your Heart on Paper: Staying Connected in a Loose-ends World.* New York: Bantam. 1995.

Knübler-Ross, Elisabeth. *On Death and Dying: What the dying have to teach doctors, nurses, clergy and their own families.* New York: The Macmillan Company. 1969.
— . *Questions and Answers on Death and Dying.* New York: Collier. 1974.

Kushner, Harold S. *When Bad Things Happen to Good People.* New York: Avon. 1981.

Lewis, C. S. *A Grief Observed.* New York: Bantam. 1961.

Levine, Stephen. *Who Dies? An Investigation of Conscious Living and Conscious Dying.* New York: Anchor Doubleday. 1982.

Miller, Jack. *Healing Our Losses: A Journal for Working Through Your Grief.* San Jose: Resource Publication, Inc. 1993.

Molloy, William and Virginia Mepham *Let Me Decide: The Health and Personal Care Directive that Speaks for You when You Can't...* Toronto: Penguin. 1996

Morgan, Ernest. *Dealing Creatively with Death: A Manual of Death Education and Simple Burial.* Bayside, NY: Zinn Communications. 1994.

Mumm, Susan M. *The Rituals Resource Book: Alternative Weddings, Funerals, Holidays and Other Rites of Passage.* Ann Arbor: Alexandra Yul Publishing & Distributing. 1995.

Munsch, Robert. *Love You Forever.* Willowdale: Firefly Books. 1986.

Panuthos, Claudia and Catherine Romeo. *Ended Beginnings: Healing Childbearing Losses.* South Hadley: Bergin & Garvey Publishers, Inc. 1984.

Pogue, Carolyn, editor. *Treasury of Celebrations: Create Celebrations that Reflect Your Values and Don't Cost the Earth.* Kelowna, BC: Northstone Publishing Inc. 1996.
— . *Unholy Poems.* Calgary: Playing for Life Publications. 1995.

Richter, Elizabeth. *Losing Someone You Love: When a Brother or Sister Dies.* New York: G.P. Putnam's Sons. 1986.

Rinpoche, Sogyai. *The Tibetan Book of Living and Dying.* New York: HarperSanFrancisco. 1992.

Rupp, Joyce. *Praying Our Goodbyes.* Notre Dame: Ave Maria Press. 1988.

Schwartzentruber, Michael. *From Crisis to New Creation: a terminally ill young man probes "All that I would like to be."* Winfield, BC: Wood Lake Books. 1986.

Searl, Edward. *In Memoriam: A Guide to Modern Funeral and Memorial Services.* Boston: Skinner House. 1993.

Stern, Ellen Sue. *Living with Loss: Meditations for Grieving Widows.* New York: Bantam Doubleday Dell Publishing Group. 1995.

Taylor, James. *Letters to Stephen: A Father's Journey of Grief and Recovery.* Kelowna, BC: Northstone Publishing Inc. 1996.

Varley, Susan. *Badger's Parting Gifts.* Glasgow: William Collins Sons & Co. Ltd. 1984.

Wall, Kathleen and Gary Ferguson. *Lights of Passage: Rituals and Rites of Passage for the Problems and Pleasures of Modern Life.* New York: HarperSanFrancisco. 1994.

Williams, Donna Reilly & JoAnn Sturzl. *Grief Ministry: Helping Others Mourn.* San Jose: Resource Publications, Inc. 1992.

Willson, Jane Wynne. *Funerals without God: A Practical Guide to Non-Religious Funerals.* New York: Prometheus Books. 1990.

Wolfelt, Alan D. *Creating Meaningful Funeral Ceremonies: A Guide for Caregivers.* Fort Collins: Companion Press. 1994.

Wylie, Betty Jane. *Beginnings: A Book for Widows.* Toronto: McClelland and Stewart. 1977.

— . *New Beginnings: Living Through Loss and Grief.* Toronto: Key Porter Books Ltd. 1991.

The HarperCollins Study Bible: New Revised Standard Version. New York: HarperCollins. 1993.

The Practical Guide for Widows. Winnipeg: Widows Consultation Centre, YM-YWCA. 1990.

Preserving Dignity: Personal Directives. Edmonton: Bioethics Centre. University of Alberta. 1996.

Services for Death and Burial for Optional Use in the United Church of Canada. Toronto: United Church Publishing House. 1987.

Kivalliq News: Voice of the Keewatin. Rankin Inlet: Northern News Services. August 1996.

The Role of the Chief Medical Examiner's Office. Manitoba Justice Department. December 1992.

Beat the High Cost of Dying: Benefits of Memorial Society Membership. Alberta Memorial Societies Co-ordinating Council.

Funerals: An Information Guide. Alberta Funeral Service Association. 1995.

Cremation Explained: Answers to Frequently Asked Questions. Funeral and Memorial Societies of America, Inc.

Music Suggested in Chapter 5:

Lullaby (for a deep sleep) by Barbara Lewis from Hara's Quest CD
Available from:
Cutting Edge Productions
2500 Cavendish Blvd
Ste 207
Montreal, Quebec H4B 2Z6
514-486-8556

On Eagle's Wings by Michael Joncas, pub by New Dawn Music

How Deep Is Your Compassion by Tracy Danz and Bob Stromberg,
pub by Stream Mountain Music

Children of the Heavenly Father and *Thy Holy Wings, Dear Saviour*,
words by Lina Sandell, Swedish folk melody, pub by Augsburg Fortress

Jesus Loves Me by Anna Bartlett Warner, pub by The Anglican Church
of Canada and United Church of Canada 1971 in *The Hymn Book*

Books of Prayer and Meditation

Fox, Matthew. *Meditations with Meister Eckhart.* Santa Fe: Bear and
Company. 1983.
— . *Meditations with Hildegard of Bingen.* Santa Fe: Bear and
Company. 1983.

Hurlow, Janet. *Psalms from the Hills of West Virginia.* Santa Fe: Bear
and Company. 1982.

Keay, Kathy. *Dancing on Mountains: An Anthology of Women's
Spiritual Writings.* London: HarperCollins. 1996.

Lavin, Edward J. *Life Meditations: Thoughts and Quotations for All of Life's Moments*. New York: Wings. 1993.

Leadingham, Carrie, et al, editors. *Peace Prayers: Meditations, Affirmations, Invocations, Poems and Prayers for Peace*. New York: HarperSanFrancisco. 1992.

Lindbergh, Anne Morrow. *Gift from the Sea*. New York: Vintage Books. 1955 and 1975.

Loder, Ted. *Guerrillas of Grace: Prayers for the Battle*. San Diego: LuraMedia. 1984.

Roberts, Elizabeth and Elias Amidon, Editors. *Earth Prayers from Around the World*. New York: HarperCollins. 1991.

Schaffran, Janet and Pat Kozak. *More Than Words: Prayer and Ritual for Inclusive Communities*. New York: Crossroad Publishing Company. 1991.

Streep, Peg, editor. *The Sacred Journey: Prayers and Songs of Native America*. Boston: Bullfinch Press and Toronto: Little Brown and Company. 1995.

Taylor, James. *Everyday Psalms: The power of the Psalms in language and images for today*. Winfield, BC: Wood Lake Books. 1994.

Weylander, Keri. *Joy is Our Banquet: Resources for Everyday Worship*. Toronto: United Church Publishing House. 1996.

Winter, Miriam Therese. *Woman Prayer Woman Song: Resources for Ritual*. New York: Crossroad. 1991.

For Support for Siblings and Parents Regarding the Death of a Child, any Age

The Compassionate Friends
Canadian National Office
685 Williams Avenue
Winnipeg, MB M3E 0Z2
The Compassionate Friends
Box 3696 Oak Brook, IL 60522-3696

For Parents who Have Experienced Neonatal Death

AMEND
Los Angeles Chapter
4032 Towhee Drive
Calabasas, CA 91302

HOPE
(Help Other Parents Endure)
c/o Susan Harrington
South Shore Hospital
55 Fogg Road
South Weymouth, MA 02190

For Parents Grieving Sudden Infant Death

SIDS Foundation
Sudden Infant Death
Ste 308
586 Eglinton Avenue E.
Toronto, ON M4P 1P2
1-800-363-7437

National Sudden Infant Death Syndrome Foundation
10500 Little Patuxent Parkway
Suite 420
Columbia, MD 21044
1-800-221-7437

Memorial Societies

Memorial Society Association of Canada
Box 46
Station A
Weston, ON M9N 3M6

Continental Association of Funeral and Memorial Societies
6900 Lost Lake Road
Egg Harbor WI 54209
414-868-3136

For Caregivers Supporting People Facing Life-threatening Illness and Bereavement

St. Francis Center
5135 Mac Arthur Blvd NW
Washington, DC 20016
202-363-8500

National Hospice Organization
1901 N. Moore Street
Ste 901
Arlington, VA 22209
703-243-5900

Children's Hospice International
700 Princess Street
Lower Level
Alexandria, VA 22314
1-800-242-4453

For Information about Suicide

Canadian Suicide Information Centre
Suite 201
1615 - 10th Avenue SW
Calgary, AB T3C 0J7
403-245-3900

American Association of Suicidology
Department of Health
2459 S. Ash
Denver, CO 80222
303-692-0985

This Silent Shame is a documentary video film on suicide and bullying.
It aired October 15, 1996 and is also available in transcript form.
Contact:
The Fifth Estate
CBC
Station A, Box 500
Toronto, ON M5W 1E6

For Information about Anatomical Gifts

The Kidney Foundation
5165 Sherbrooke Street W.
Ste 300
Montreal, PQ H4A 1T6

National Kidney Foundation
30 East 33rd Street
New York, NY 10016
1-800-662-9010

Eye Bank Association of America
1001 Connecticut Ave NW
Washington, DC 20036-5504
202-775-4999

Eye Bank of Canada
The Canadian Institute for the Blind
1929 Fairview Avenue
Toronto, ON M4G 3E8

Organ Donors Canada
5326 Ada Boulevard
Edmonton, AB T5W 4N7
403-474-9363

Silent Hearts Inc
The Australian Organ Donor Family Organization
Box 839
Bowral NSW 2576
048-871-243
email:lhuntsma@mail.usyd.edu.au

The Ear Bank of Project HEAR
801 Welch Road
Palo Alto, CA 94304
415-494-2000

Ear Bank of British Columbia
865 W 10th Avenue
Vancouver, BC V5Z 1L7
250-876-3211 ext 3212

To Donate Eyeglasses

New Eyes for the Needy
Box 332
549 Milburn Avenue
Short Hills NJ 07078
201-376-4093

Operation Eyesight Universal
4 Parkdale Cres NW
Calgary, AB T2N 3T8
403-283-6323

For General Bereavement Support

Bereavement: a Magazine of Hope and Healing
Bereavement Publishing Inc.
8133 Telegraph Drive
Colorado Springs, CO 80920-7069

Rainbows Offers a Grief Support Curricula for Children, Adolescents
and Young Adults in 12 Countries.
RAINBOWS USA
111 Tower Road
Schaumburg, IL 60173
1-800-266-3206
Fax: 847-310-0120
Web site: http://www.RAINBOWS.ORG

RAINBOWS CANADA
Thelma Cockburn
17 Theresa Street
Barrie, ON L4M 1J5
Phone: 705-726-7407
Fax: 705-726-5805

APPENDIX B:
SUGGESTED SCRIPTURE READINGS

Hebrew Scriptures

Numbers 6:24-26 (May the Lord bless you and keep you.)

Job 19:1, 21-27a (My Redeemer lives, in spite of all)

   28:20-28 (Where is wisdom and understanding?)

Psalm 23 (The Lord is my shepherd.)

   27 (The Lord is my light and salvation.)

   42 (Longing for God's help in distress.)

   46 (God is our refuge and strength.)

   90:1-6 (A thousand years in God's sight are like yesterday when it is past.)

   98 (Sing to the Lord a new song; let the floods clap their hands.)

   117 (Universal call to worship.)

   121 ((The Lord will keep your going out and coming in forever.)

   130 (I cry to God and rely on God's steadfast love.)

   139:1-18, 23-24 (You, God, knit me together in my mother's womb; lead me in the everlasting way.)

Proverbs 31:10-31 (The capable wife)

Ecclesiastes 3:1-15 (There is a time for everything.)

Song of Solomon 8:6-7 (Power of love)

Isaiah 25:6-9 (God will prepare a banquet; God will swallow death.)

   40:1-11 (Comfort, comfort O my people!)

   46:3-4 (I, God, am with you from womb to old age.)

   61:1-3 (Comfort to all who mourn.)

Lamentations 3:17-24 (My soul is bereft, but God's love and mercy never end.)

Hosea 6:1a and 3 (God will come to us like the spring rains.)

Micah 6:6-8 (What does the Lord require? Justice, kindness, walk humbly with God.)

Wisdom of Solomon 3:1-4 & 9 (The souls of the righteous are in the hand of God.)

New Testament

Matthew 5:1-10 (The Beatitudes)

6:25-34 (Don't worry about tomorrow; concentrate on today.)

11:28-30 (Come to me all you who are weary and are carrying heavy burdens.)

18:1-5 (True greatness is like a child.)

25:34-40 (When I was hungry, you gave me food; when I was thirsty...)

Mark 9:2-8 (The Transfiguration of Jesus.)

15:33-44 (Jesus is crucified and dies.)

Luke 23:39-56 (Jesus is crucified with criminals; Joseph of Arimathea buries him.)

24:1-10, 13-16, 28-36 (Angels tell the women Jesus is risen; Jesus appears to the men.)

John 6:35-39 (I am the bread of life; whoever comes to me will never be hungry.)

11:21-36 (Martha and Jesus talk about death at the tomb of Lazarus; Jesus weeps for his friend.)

14:1-4 (Jesus tells the disciples he is going to prepare a place for them.)

20:11-18 (Resurrected Jesus appears to Mary Magdalene.)

Acts 10:34-41 (Peter preaches about Jesus and says he was resurrected by God.)

1 Corinthians 13:1-13 (The gift of love; love is patient, kind, rejoices in truth and never ends.)

15:51-55 (The dead will be resurrected; death has been swallowed up in victory.)

Ephesians 3:16-21 (Paul prays that God will grant strength and comprehension to the Ephesians.)

Philippians 4:4-9 (Take everything to God in prayer, don't worry, may the peace of God guard your hearts.)

Hebrews 11:1-3 (Faith is the assurance of things hoped for; by it we understand the invisible is made visible.)

1 Peter 1:3-5 (By God's mercy we have hope through the resurrection of Jesus and into an imperishable inheritance.)

Revelation 21:1-7 (A vision of a new Heaven and a new Earth where God wipes away every tear and death, mourning, crying and pain will be no more.)

22:1-5 (A vision of the river of the water of life and the tree of life; the leaves of the tree are for the healing of the nations.)

Suggested Prayers in the Presence of One who is Dying

Almighty God, look on this your servant, lying in great weakness, and comfort him/her with the promise of life everlasting, given in the resurrection of your Son Jesus Christ our Lord. Amen.

The Lord's Prayer, or the following may be said with the dying person:

Glory be to the Father, and to the Son, and to the Holy Spirit: as it was in the beginning, is now, and ever shall be, world without end. Amen.

God of mercy, look with love on N. and receive him/her into your heavenly kingdom. Bless him/ her and let him/her live with you for ever. We ask this grace through Christ our Lord. Amen.

Prayer at Death

Depart, O Christian soul, out of this world, in the name of God the Father Almighty who created thee; in the name of Jesus Christ who

redeemed thee; in the name of the Holy Spirit, who sanctifieth thee. May thy rest be this day in peace and thy dwelling-place in the Paradise of God.
– from *Canadian Church Diary 1997*, Anglican Book Centre, 600 Jarvis Street, Toronto, Canada M4Y 2J6

Readings and Prayers at the Time of Death

Suggested readings:
Psalm 23, Psalm 46, Psalm 121, Luke 2:29-32.

Hands may be placed on the head or hand of the dying person as the prayer is said:
Almighty God, by your power you raised Jesus Christ from death. Watch over this child/servant of yours, our sister/brother *(name)*. Fill her/his eyes with light, that she/he may see beyond human sight a home within your love where pain is gone and frailty becomes glory. Banish fear. Brush away tears. May sighs of grief turn to songs of joy in the presence of Jesus Christ our Lord. Amen.

At Death

Depart in peace in the name of God Most Holy who created you; in the name of God the Son, Jesus Christ, who redeemed you; in the name of God the Holy Spirit who sanctifies you. May you rest this day/night in peace, and dwell forever in God's care. Amen.

Into your hands, O merciful Savior, we commend your servant *(name)*. Acknowledge, we humbly pray, a sheep of your own fold, a lamb of your own flock, and a daughter/son of your own redeeming. Receive her/him into the arms of your mercy, into the blessed rest of everlasting peace, and into the glorious company of the saints in light. Amen.

from *Services for Death and Burial: for optional use in*
The United Church of Canada,
The United Church of Canada, Toronto, Ontario

Index

A

ashes 51
autopsy 40

B

benedictions 94, 118
body (the)
    bequeathal of 53
        to medical science 53
    dressing of 48
    washing of 48
burial 42, 146
    shroud 42
    vaults 44

C

caskets 45, 85
    choosing a 85
    costs 47
    homemade 45
cemeteries 42-3
    plots 42
ceremonies
    planning 71
    sample
        A Celebration of Courage (for
        transplant recipients and donor
        families) 167
        For a Child 114
        One-Year Survival (after suicide)
        129
        Ritual for Pregnancy Loss 107
        Ritual of Letting Go (when the
        relationship was bad) 96
        Ritual of Remembrance 92
        Service of Committal (for pregnancy
        loss) 106
    sample outline 77-82
        closing 82
        committal 82
        meditation/sermon 75, 82
ceremonies
    sample outline cont'd
        music 78

        personal tributes 80
        prayer(s) 78
        readings 78
        welcome 78
children (at funerals) 22, 76, 84, 94, 110
coffins, *see caskets*
Committal Service for Pregnancy Loss 106
community 21
    healing of 28
    importance of 21, 27
cremation 39, 45, 51-53, 147
crematorium 52

D

death 17, 35, 135
    and grief 26
    at home 36
    denial of 17
    in a foreign country 37
    in institutions 17
    of a baby 109
    of a child 101, 110
    your own 135
        cremation 147
        disposal of body 146
        funeral memorial ceremony 144
        living wills, personal directives 140
death certificate 40
dressing
    the body 48

E

embalming 44
eulogy, *see personal tribute*
executor 155

F

feelings 23
flowers 86
Flying Funeral Directors of
    [North] America 40
funeral directors 22, 40
    role of 39

funeral homes 38, 41, 59
   choosing a 39
funerals 21, 38, 76, 144-145, see also
   ceremonies
    average cost 41
    in North America 21
    purpose of 26
    travel/discounts 41
    without a funeral home 65-69
    worksheet 99

G
graveyards 43
grief 26

H
headstones 43
Holocaust Memorial 30

I
intestate death 155

L
Living Wills 140

M
music 78
meditation 82
memorial service 38, 99, 144, 146
memorial societies 54, 138
mourning 55

O
obituary 50, 87
One-Year Survival Ceremony
    (after suicide) 129
organ donation 159

P
pall 42
personal directives 140
personal tributes 74, 80-81
photographs 86
power of attorney 156
prayers 78
   for comfort 117
   opening 130

pregnancy loss 103
PreNeed Funeral Plans 55
probate 154

R
readings 74-75, 78, 93, 106, 130, 133
refreshments 89
Ritual for Pregnancy Loss 107
Ritual of letting go 96
Ritual of Remembrance (when the relationship was bad) 94
rituals 19
   at moment of death 35
   community involvement 21
   importance of 19
   use of flowers in 20

S
sermon 75, 76, 82
service folder 89
shroud 42
simplicity 30
suicide 119
symbols 74, 86

T
transplants 159

U
urns 45, 85
   homemade 46

V
values
   personal 27
Vietnam War Memorial 30
viewing
   the body 49
voluntary simplicity 19

W
welcome 78
washing
   the body 48
Wills 152